An idyllic summer encounter suddenly falters . . .

Richard rose and took a few deliberate pokes at the logs; he needed to look away and take in this strange information. So, she knew Rena, had visited her . . . What would this lovely young woman think if she knew that he was the son of a bitter, drunken woman living in that foreboding stone house?

"They say she drinks too much, that nothing good can come to those who get involved with her and her affairs." Was he really saying this? And more words sounded in his ears. "You ought to stay away from that house, you know. There's something sinister about—"

He stopped himself, seeing the sudden alarm in Angie's eyes. He laughed nervously and shrugged off his words as though they had been a joke. A very poor joke, he thought.

MARLENE J. CHASE is a regular contributor to several Christian periodicals. A major in The Salvation Army, Mrs. Chase now teaches homiletics and literature at The Salvation Army School for Officers' Training in Chicago.

Books by Marlene J. Chase

HEARTSONG PRESENTS

HP6—The Other Side of Silence

This Trembling Cup

Marlene J. Chase

Heartsong Presents

ISBN 1-55748-328-0

THIS TREMBLING CUP

PRINTED IN U.S.A.

one

No more, no more
The worldly shore
Upbraids me with its loud uproar
With dreamful eyes
My spirit lies
Under the walls of Paradise!

THOMAS BUCHANAN READ

The aroma of pine and cedar blended with wild honeysuckle as Angie stepped outside the little cabin at Pinewood Acres Resort. Her best friend, Jen, slept inside; she was still weary from the long drive to their vacation spot, this green profusion of lush woods banking a lake so immaculately blue that it seemed to ache with beauty. A lone canoeist rode the quiet currents in the blue basin, and on the rim of an emerald hill across the lake the sun rose like the first dawn over Eden.

Angie Carlson stepped to the water's edge where newly washed stones shimmered among mahogany reeds and cattails. Small creatures darted just beneath the warm surface, their bodies glistening and green. Butterflies, their wings gilt like gold, lingered on wild morning glories then fluttered heavily away, drunk on the sweetness of the flowers. "All's right with the world," the poet's words came to her mind.

Suddenly there was a rushing in the reeds. With a frightened croak, a frog leaped away, leaving its pursuer, a silvery lizard, panting and bewildered.

Then into Angie's heart they sprang, the broken ones in their squalid darkness. No poet's blissful sentiment could have issued from their bleak hearts. *I don't want to think of them now,* she mused. It was her vacation, a time to heal wounds of the battle waged over poverty, ignorance, and inhumanity.

When Angie had first taken the position as youth pastor at an inner-city church, she had been full of a sense of sureness and power. These were people who needed her. She could face the sullenness, the hunger, and the pathos of those youthful eyes. She could lift them, show them a better way, and love them in spite of their anger, an anger that she knew was borne of great physical and spiritual deprivation.

Now nearly four years had passed, four desperate years with little to show that she had lived among them. She had poured out her energy, her intellect, and her heart. What few strides had been made were nothing in the vast network of despair and need that surrounded her and the youth of that community.

She blinked her eyes, wishing to erase these pathetic ones from her memory. She watched the ripples caused by the frog's sudden flight slowly disperse and traced her own reflection on the water. Light brown hair, too light to be brown, too dark to be blond, circled her face like the intricate feathering of wind-swept sand. Brown eyes tinged with gold, beneath delicately arched brows, stared back at her. She traced the slender lines of her nose and soft, slightly trembling mouth. She didn't look much like a youth pastor, she decided; she looked more like those yearning, fearful ones she had loved so much. The trouble was, loving them hadn't been enough.

The people who haunted her now all seemed to coalesce into the figure of one small enigmatic child named Eddie. His face filled her mind now as she watched the widening ripples on the lake. The watery image with its speckles of light and shadow gave way to a darker, disturbing vision, one she knew too well. It had been little more than a week ago that she had prepared for the children's arrival.

She had come early for Sunday school. Eight o'clock was not exactly the crack of dawn, but there, where life seemed to come to a nightly crisis, the neighborhood lay spent, encased in a fragile, morning peace. Scraps of old newspaper swirled at her feet, and an empty bottle of Jack Daniels lay like a spent grenade on a field of battle. She knew that she shouldn't be surprised. Still, the strewn paper and empty bottle struck her with a sense of hopelessness as she considered the people she had tried to care for. She had bled with them, and had bound up wounds, but few of those she touched were any different than before.

While unpacking the contents of her briefcase in the little office there was a crash and a tinkle of glass spraying on the hardwood floor in the adjoining chapel. She had heard that sound before, but still her stomach reeled and her breath caught somewhere in her chest. She shouldn't be here alone, she thought. The early morning was so much a part of the night. They had warned her. But she needed to be here, to pray, to listen, before they came.

Shuddering, she remembered that Reverend Packett's

wife had once been struck with a bottle and left bleeding on that very same floor. The thug had stolen her wedding ring, a ring worth less than thirty-five dollars to any local fence.

She waited, but there was no further sound. Swallowing her fear she walked into the chapel, her shoes clacking over the uncarpeted floor. A jagged hole gaped in the front window on the east side of the church, and on the floor among the shattered fragments of glass lay the smooth, round rock. She stood in dismay. It was one of only two windows that had not already been replaced with unbreakable Plexiglas. It must be him again!

She ran to the rear door and flung herself out, unmindful of her high heels and her long-sleeved blouse pulling loose from her waist. The small, fenced parking lot lay empty and the streets deserted except for the ever-present litter. She spun around the corner of the building, sure to find him. How many times he had promised!

She stood with her hands on her slender hips and waited, her anger building. She had tried everything with him. The empty streets seemed to mock her as her frustration grew. Then a great weariness quickly washed over her like the gray mist of smog-heavy air. Realizing that the vandal had fled, she went back inside, mechanically got the broom and dustpan from the supply closet, and began sweeping up.

She knew the moment he came. Not looking up, she kept sweeping with short, brisk strokes. The glass splinters glimmered oddly like fine crystal in the shaft of light coming through the hole.

"Who did that, lady?" a boy's voice came in strange, guttural accents. "Huh? Who did it?"

She stopped sweeping and looked into the thin face of eight-year-old Eddie Loss. Why must he call her "lady"? After all these months why couldn't he call her "Sister Angeline" like everyone else?

Angie swept the glass fragments into the dustpan and faced the boy. He stood, a sallow child with a round little belly that stuck out above pencil-thin legs in cutoff shorts. The legs ended in a pair of laceless shoes that flopped on his feet, their tongues hanging out like hounddogs' tongues after a chase.

Her eyes traveled to his face, a bony oval with enormous protruding ears. His thatch of hair stood up like a mound of straw left outside to winter. His eyes, not menacing or sorrowful, shone in the early sun with an aura of perpetual glee.

His eyes were always like that, whether he was being scolded, implored, or praised. Over the time she had known him there had been little reason to praise him. Dirty, unmannerly, and troublesome, he had already broken most of the windows in the mission at least once.

"I did it, lady," he said, pointing a finger to his chest and parting his lips to reveal stained, uneven teeth.

She shook her head, watching him. Why didn't he just do it and run like any other boy would? Why stand there with such a look of pleasure about himself and plead guilty? Didn't he understand? Was he proud of the dubious distinction of having broken most of the windows in the little church? Something in her melted.

She knew Eddie, knew that he came from a home where the mother was too ill and too tired to raise her children. She knew that the children had once been taken from the home by protective service officials, only to be returned again. She knew Eddie got himself up in the morning, searched for his own breakfast, and spent his days on the street. It wouldn't be long before he was hopelessly enmeshed in something far more dreadful than breaking windows.

"Eddie, why did you break the window again?" she asked quietly.

He responded with a grand shrug of fragile shoulders, a grin. Then came the promise with a dramatic toss of his head. "I won't do it again, lady, okay?" The boy shrugged and fumbled with a handful of bottle caps, switching them from one grimy hand to another.

Suddenly he brightened. "I'm going to go to the carnival," he said, as though the discussion about the window were finished.

The carnival, held each summer in the inner city, was sponsored by the Chamber of Commerce. "Eddie," she began.

"I'm gonna' ride the horses, and go round the big pole!"

She watched him helplessly. What would happen to him? He wasn't cute or smart or lucky. He was part boy, part merry elf who only wished to romp through the world among beautiful, intriguing things and to be happy. How soon would he find out that the world is neither a safe nor happy place in which to romp?

"Eddie, I know you'll have fun at the carnival. But you must not break people's windows. I'll have to speak to your mother about it again."

His small shoulders rolled and fell again. He dumped the bottle caps back into his pocket as a little shadow of sadness darkened his eyes. Then suddenly he spied something floating in a beam of sunlight. He cupped his hands and stepped in his floppy shoes to catch it. It eluded him, and he went after it again. Then he chased it to the door of the mission.

"Bye, lady," he called as he skipped away. His elfish face shimmered briefly, then faded away in the settling water of Pinewood Acres private lake.

But all that was over. Now Angie Carlson was 200 miles away from the grime of the inner city and from the haunting eyes of little Eddie. Or was she?

She bent to touch the petals of a lily that wavered pink and fleshy on a fragile stem. She pulled it, and, like the delicate dreams of innocence, it came up, easily unmoored. She studied her fingernails against the soft green stem. She had had so little time to take care of things like cuticles and nails. Now two weeks were hers to enjoy, away from broken bottles and the smell of stale sweat. She would be just plain Angie, not Miss Angie or Sister Angeline. She wasn't sure she knew how to be that person anymore.

She and Jen had set off early yesterday afternoon, as soon as her duties were finished at the mission. She had bid Reverend Packett farewell, deliberately avoiding the perceptive eyes of Mrs. Packett. Had she somehow sensed the despair, the half-framed resolve, on the part of a disappointed, ineffective leader not to come back? Wouldn't it be better for them all if she did not return?

The city from which she and Jen had fled in midafternoon stared after them like a wounded beast with a thousand sightless eyes. Soon it grew faint and forgotten in the distance as their journey wore on. The road stretched long and they drove leisurely. Ancient guardian fields swept low, bowing and scraping like royal grenadiers paying tribute to queens.

Jen, tall, big-boned, with hips that tended slightly to largeness, had been Angie's friend since college days. With her smooth, dark skin that responded to the sun's rays like tomatoes left to ripen on a kitchen window sill and her frank blue eyes, she gave every sense of stability and worth. She could crank a jack and whip bolts off with a tire wrench like a swarthy mechanic, but she could also comfort a distressed child with the gentle softness of an angel. She taught school in the same city where Angie worked. They had been good for each other. Angie couldn't imagine how she would have survived without the comfort of this special friend.

Because of this friend they were vacationing at the plush resort owned by Jen's aunt. Each cabin surrounding the lake boasted small but charming features, including a kitchenette and a fireplace supplied with fresh firewood every evening. A sandy beach, boating and fishing facilities, tennis courts, and a rolling, eighteen-hole golf course answered the recreational needs of the resort's guests. Known to be one of the finest resorts in northern Wisconsin, Pinewood Acres was financially out of reach for both of them.

"It's really super of your aunt to let us come," Angie had said as they drew near the fashionably quaint resort. "We'd never be able to afford it at the real price."

"Aunt Rena was always generous, if a little foolhardy, but lately," she paused and drummed her fingers on the steering wheel as she always did when something was bothering her, "lately, we've been a little worried about her."

"Why?"

"Well, she's always had a bit of a wild streak in her, but Mom says she's been drinking too much, more than ever. And believe me, she always drank too much. Ah, no matter. You don't want to hear about it."

Angie drew in a deep breath. Perhaps not. She'd had enough of the trauma of substance abuse and its helpless victims. But Jen was still protecting her, as though she were a wounded child. Perhaps she was. "No, tell me about it, Jen," Angie said softly. "What's your Aunt Rena like?"

"None of us was ever very close to Aunt Rena. She always sent us nice presents, but she never had time to spend with us. Always off on some adventure! Like this resort she purchased some years ago after a big investment paid off for her. Actually, she has a manager to run this place. She's had a string of them, really. They never stay long with her. Then there's Miss Kremser, the woman Aunt Rena hired to clean and help with her correspondence. I hear she just about runs things now."

"Doesn't your aunt have any children to look after her?" Angie asked absently, entranced by the sight of slender white birches as supple as dancers, the leaves like bangles on slender wrists.

"A son," Jen replied matter-of-factly. "My cousin Rick. He left when he was only seventeen. He never got along very well with Aunt Rena. Actually, I hadn't heard much about him until recently. He's been asking about Rena, and about the financial trouble with the resort." Jen paused, frowning. "I guess my aunt won't have anything to do with him."

"Maybe he's trying to make amends for the early years," Angie suggested. "Maybe he really does care about her—"

"Or her money," Jen said quickly and then shrugged. "But then, you could put what I know about Rick in a thimble. I guess we're not exactly what you'd call a close family." She became quiet then, and something of profound sadness shadowed her face. "Funny how you can live whole summers together and still be strangers," she laughed. "Rick always beat me at every game. Downright humiliating it was!"

Now, as Angie walked slowly along the edge of the water, she lifted her face to the skies, breathing in the freshness of the new morning. She didn't want to think about Jen's family and about this strange Aunt Rena who owned the resort. She didn't want to see Eddie's face or the faces of the others who haunted her peace. She longed for the freedom of wind and water, the peace of summer sunshine, and the joy of a single pink lily on a fragile stem. These were things that didn't need her or ask for something she could not give.

two

> This life which seems so fair
> is like a bubble blown up in the air
> By sporting children's breath
> who chase it everywhere . . . .
>
> W. Drummond

The path along the water ended in a marshy plain that led to a tree-covered bluff where branches lopped and tangled in a plethora of gold and green. As she entered the small forest on the hill, a silence touched her, a silence like the abrupt ending of a symphony and the startled stillness before a listening crowd applauds. She walked into the little cove and stood enraptured beneath birches whose slender trunks leaned toward one another, forming a sort of primal cathedral.

Looking down she could see the dawn spilling into the arms of the lake below, and from her shadowed refuge she seemed somehow estranged from it, as though she beheld creation from some untouchable galaxy. An awed grieving came over her. "The woods are lovely, dark and deep," Robert Frost's poem echoed in her mind as she sat down on a decaying log to rest. Pine needles had fallen in silent burial to the forest floor, and their brown deadness touched her with singular sadness. "Promises to keep?" she wondered.

Here she had come to greet the morning, to meditate and pray as was her custom at the start of each day. But now, only the echoing phrase "promises to keep" repeated itself in her mind, and with it came the memory of other woods and a campfire and a burning.

She had been so young. It seemed an eternity ago, and yet it touched her now as a presence in the cove. She had gone on a church retreat with her friends, a campfire program where she sat watching the fire, identifying her own life with the dying embers. As the group leader stirred the embers with a long stick, sparks flew upward as though ignited by some great power. The vibrant flames widened, climbed! In that instant she identified the fire with the purifying touch of God, and it seemed her lips burned with His fire.

She had given herself wholly in service to this One who had so changed her life, and had given her such a sense of joy and love. She paused, remembering how things had been before. In her earliest memories she recalled a strange sense of alienation: Mother leaving early for work and a string of babysitters to watch over her, all urging her to go away and play, with preoccupied looks on their faceless faces.

Dad had his visitation rights. She had always waited for him, had wondered why he couldn't stay. Maybe if she were really, really good. . . . Somewhere between wakefulness and sleep she would become aware of him and a sweet longing would sweep over her. Sometimes he touched her forehead. Sometimes he'd talk to her, his dark eyes twinkling. Then he was gone, leaving that sweet-sour reminiscence of wine.

This separation continued throughout her childhood. Then the news of his death came, and with it, a nameless emotion, deeper than loss, stronger than love. Somehow she should have been able to change things. She should have been able to make him well so that he would come home and they would be a real family again.

Angie picked a tiny yellow flower, incongruous amid the decay and dry death of the rotting log on which she sat. Not until she was sixteen did she learn of the Father who really loved her, who loved her enough to stay! And she learned of God's power to heal the human spirit. Joyfully she vowed to serve Him who had shown her such love. "Promises to keep. . . ."

And yet, her efforts had been fruitless. Had she been mistaken? Perhaps she wasn't cut out for this life. She had never thought it would be like this: the constant struggle, the failure. She remembered the promised talk with Eddie's mother about the windows. The talk, the useless talk, hadn't prevented the terrible thing that she still couldn't frame in her mind.

On that morning she had made her way to the shabby building where a fire escape rose wearily up to a dilapidated second story. Drapes were knotted to admit air into stale rooms. At the back entrance two little boys played on the stairs, shoving tawdry cars back and forth along the rotting wood. She knocked on the screen door that flapped back and forth like a wounded bird on useless wings.

"It's open," a woman's voice responded dully.

Mrs. Sandra Loss sat, both hands clutching a stained coffee cup, her face registering neither gladness nor surprise. Perhaps she had once been a pretty woman, Angie thought. Faded blond hair partially restrained by a yellow ribbon surrounded a well-shaped face with intensely dark eyes, in sharp contrast to the stark whiteness of her face. Her stomach, weak from frequent childbearing, protruded oddly beneath puffy hands. She looked like a woman grown suddenly old. She shoved her coffee cup onto a low table littered with dishes, newspapers, and a vase of dusty plastic roses.

"Please, you don't need to get up," Angie said. "How are you feeling today?"

The woman shrugged, reminding Angie of Eddie. "I had a treatment yesterday at the clinic. Sure tires a body out."

Angie swallowed against the lump in her throat. Cancer. Those dreadful treatments often left patients sick and worn out. "I'm sorry."

The television exploded with raucous laughter and the bantering of a game-show host. Sandra made no move to turn off the set or to lower the volume. She fixed her eyes on the dancing screen where someone exulted over winning a new automobile and an all-expenses-paid trip to the Bahamas. The clapping and screaming filled the room. Then came the commercial: a little girl in football gear running up to the closet of a plush suburban home for toilet paper.

"You came about Eddie, didn't you?" Sandra asked, not looking at Angie, her eyes following the commercial.

"Yes. I'm sorry to bother you, but . . ."

"Another window?"

"Yes." She paused, wishing there were something positive to say. "Eddie doesn't . . . well, he doesn't seem to understand. He breaks the windows, then he very nicely tells me about it and promises not to do it again. But—"

"But he does it again," Sandra finished lamely, not taking her eyes off the television.

"Yes. He must stop destroying property." Angie knotted her hands in frustration. She hadn't gone about this right.

"I know. Eddie thinks everything in life is one big game made just for him." Here the deep eyes looked beyond to some unseen image. Something of beauty or youth lay there ever so briefly, and then was gone. "I reckon he'll learn soon enough it ain't much of a game."

Angie paused, wondering if it was the right thing to say, but the words tumbled out. "Better he learn from you than from someone who doesn't care if he wins or loses."

"I'll talk to him again," she said softly. "Roslyn, his sister, will keep a stricter eye on him." She gave a deep sigh. "I . . . I know you've been good to my Eddie, and the others. I'm sorry about the windows."

Angie rose to leave. "Goodbye, Mrs. Loss. I hope you're feeling better soon." She paused, feeling desolate. She had asked before and been turned down, but maybe this time. . . . "Mrs. Loss, I'd be happy to pray with you before—"

"No." The eyes turned back to the television screen. "Thanks for your trouble, but no." The voice was more rigid than at any other time in their conversation. Angie left the shabby house with leaden heart.

Then, a few days later, on a sultry Thursday midnight, the inexplicable horror, had occurred. When it was over and there was no longer any need for talks about windows and the silent little body was finally at rest, she had taken the counsel of Reverend and Mrs. Packett and had made plans with Jen for a vacation. Jen had somehow carried her over those few days after the horror.

But one must say something to the most broken one who must remain to remember. So she had paid a second call on Sandra Loss.

"I'll be away for a couple weeks," she had told Sandra,

but if the grieving mother had heard she didn't know. Was that the truth? Would she come back? "If you need anything, please let Reverend Packett know. I—" But what was left to be said? She clasped Sandra's cold hands and smiled into the unresponsive face. And that had been her last encounter before leaving the dreadful city behind.

Now, as Angie sat on the old log in the little cover of trees, she brooded over the episode. She had so wanted to make some difference in the lives of those hurting people, to show them a little light in the midst of their darkness. Sighing, she rose from the log and fixed her eyes on the open space between the trees that arched over her head. Lifting her arms she grasped the birch limb and stared sadly into the little patch of sky.

She began to sing a song that had no words that she knew, a plaintive melody that issued from the deepest longings of her heart and from the wounded center of her spirit that longed for healing.

Suddenly she stopped. A small crackling sound, like branches pulled back and let go. Were there steps? She whirled about. Only the trees and the dead log and the silence. She waited, suddenly afraid—no, not afraid—but vulnerable, embarrassed that some secret might have been discovered.

She walked farther up the bluff; the spaces between the trees grew and more sunlight shone in. Presently she came to the top and saw a stone house sprawling high and wide, its presence severe and foreboding even with the sun shining full on its gray sides and black rolled roof. Its windows peered like dark eyes from its smoky countenance, and Angie felt a shudder run through her like a delayed electric shock.

Rena's house, the twelve-room mansion of the owner of Pinewood Acres, seemed not a part of the resort at all, but remote and detached, as though lingering over some coveted prize that it would seize in the night and draw to itself. A wide verandalike porch loomed at the front of the house, its great stone pillars rising in the sky like Stonehenge. Evergreens spired on the grounds around it, circling like a timber moat around a castle.

"She keeps to herself. She likes it that way," Jen had told her.

Angie shuddered and turned away, aware once again of the strange sense of being observed. Her skin tingled and went cold. But that was absurd, she told herself. Grass and trees and sky loomed about her, warm, engaging, benign. Shivering in spite of the steadily warming sun, she retraced her steps down from the bluff, through the forest path, and along the lake. Fishermen had ventured out now, and their little boats almost motionless on the water reassured her.

A morning jogger raced along the path, his fashionable shorts and running shoes reminiscent of familiar, everyday things. He raised a hand in greeting, and Angie waved back, suddenly feeling better, as though she had closed a disturbing chapter of a book and come back to familiar, if unsatisfying, reality.

Inside the cabin Jen stirred orange juice with a plastic spatula. "Still the little morning adventurer, aren't you?" she said. "The only kind of adventure I want at six in the morning is a cozy dream."

Angie took a drink of the juice and set the glass down thoughtfully. "I saw your aunt's house."

"Good grief! You went clear up there?" Jen whirled around in her jersey nightshirt. She looked like a teenybopper at a pajama party.

"Well, I didn't know it was there. That is, I didn't intend to go there. I was in the cove and enjoying everything so much." She started to mention hearing something and sensing someone's presence, but she thought better of it. Jen was already worried enough about her after all that had happened. "I decided to climb farther up on the bluff, and that's when I saw it." She fell silent.

"Big old place, isn't it?" Jen said, biting into a piece of toast.

"You been there, Jen?" Angie asked casually.

"Nope. Frankly, Aunt Rena makes it pretty plain that she doesn't want visitors. Besides, that place gives me the creeps."

Angie shivered. "I know what you mean."

"I promised the folks I'd look in on her. Can't say I'm looking forward to paying that visit, though." Jennifer Flurry narrowed her dark eyes, and a rosy flush appeared on her tawny skin. "But not today! Today I want to get my swimming suit on and hit the water."

They spent the day on the beach, soaking up the sun, swimming, and dozing away their first day of vacation. They both needed this time to relax.

"It was wonderful to feel the sand under my feet," Jen said, back at the cabin. "If only we could find a place to eat dinner tonight where shoes are *not* required!" Hardly had her words been spoken when a knock sounded on their cabin door.

"There's a message at the office for Miss Jennifer Flurry. Urgent, they said." A pudgy, balding man held the screen door open for Jen.

Angie matched Jen's enigmatic glance and watched her follow the caretaker. Something in the slope of his fat shoulders and the glint of the sun on his bald spot suddenly struck her with a sense of alarm.

When Jen returned tears were forming in the dark depths of her eyes. "A heart attack. My Dad."

Angie put her arms around her friend, and something cold and clutching leaped in her stomach. "Oh, no, Jen. Oh! I'm so sorry."

"I've got to go to them."

Angie had never met Jen's parents. Indeed only now did she become aware that they existed in some reality beyond the cold photograph Jen kept on the mantel in her apartment.

Jen straightened. "Mom and Dad have never had this kind of experience. They'll need me now."

"But your vacation. It's spoiled!" Angie said, her own eyes filling with tears.

"And yours too. Oh, Angie, I'll have to leave you here all alone."

"It's all right. You go, and don't worry."

"I don't know when I'll get back. I don't know how bad things really are."

"Do you want me to go with you?"

"No." Jen flashed her a quick, genuine smile. "Spoil two vacations for the price of one?" she asked, her eyebrows arching above narrowed eyes. "Certainly not. But, will you be all right?"

"Of course. I'll be fine. You know me. I'll enjoy painting and reading and . . ." Angie hesitated. She would be without wheels. They had driven in Jen's car. She rushed on to allay her friend's further distress. "There's always the resort bus service into town, you know, if I want to go shopping or something. I'll be fine! But, Jen, please call me and let me know how things are."

"I will." Jen paused and pursed her lips thoughtfully. "I hate to ask you, but could you look in on Aunt Rena for me? I know Mom would want her to know about dad's heart attack, but I don't want to take the time to visit her right now. I want to get going!"

"Sure. Don't give it another thought."

She paused at the door of her maroon Escort. "I hate to ask you. I told you how Aunt Rena is. I hope she won't be rude to you."

"Don't worry. I can handle it."

Angie watched Jen drive away into the night, watched until the red taillights faded into oblivion like two eyes of a dying animal.

That night Angie lay awake a long time listening to the crying of the loons, the heavy drone of cicadas and crickets. So this was the way it was to be, she thought; no Jen to share pleasant times. Maybe things would go well at home and Jen could return for at least part of their vacation. But if things didn't go well, it might mean two weeks alone in this faraway place with its aching beauty, its whispered secrets.

It wasn't that she feared being alone; she was acquainted with single life. But there would be nothing to distract her from the awful memories and from finding out who she had become. She tried to pray as the lonely sounds echoed in her heart, asking for something she couldn't really articulate. Soon she was lulled into an uneasy sleep.

three

At the mid hour of night,
when stars are weeping, I fly
To the lone vale we loved,
When life shone warm in thine eye.

THOMAS MOORE

Richard Ogden pulled into the circular driveway of Pinewood Acres Resort and jumped out of the idling car. Best not to give himself time to change his mind, he thought quickly. Tossing his coat onto the seat., he stretched and found his cramped muscles relaxing. The tightness in his chest didn't ease up, though, and he wished he were almost any place but here.

He paused only a second at the pine-framed glass doors, fixing his blue-eyed gaze somewhere beyond the orange and yellow plethora of marigolds and zinnias crowding angular planters at both sides of the entrance. The sun, just beginning to set, highlighted touches of fine silver in his blond hair and beard and outlined the high plane of his tanned forehead and the slender straightness of his nose.

He paused with his hand on the door, then quickly stepped inside the carpeted foyer. Early American couches and chairs of tasteful design sat with waiting arms, and the room, not yet lit for the evening, held a dusky, sedate aura, somewhat out of place here in the north country, home of lumberjacks and hunters. Nothing too backwoodsy about this place. It wouldn't have been Rena's way.

"Evening. Richard Ogden," he said, introducing himself to

the small, stoop-shouldered man behind the desk. "I have a reservation."

"Oh, yes, your secretary phoned yesterday."

"That's correct." He wondered if Rena had taken time to look at the reservation list. Probably not. And Riggs, the manager, wouldn't be in until morning. Perhaps they didn't much monitor who came, as long as the bill was paid. He put his credit card on the counter, giving it a light meditative tap.

The man behind the desk handed Richard a key and walked to the window. "Follow the road up the westerly drive—there," he indicated with a pudgy finger. "Turn left at the end of the road." As if the words exhausted him, he nodded and sank into his desk chair.

"Thanks." Richard paused. "Mrs. Rena Mara still own this place?" he asked nonchalantly.

The eyes behind filmy glasses narrowed, then a brief nod of the balding head. "You a salesman? If so, you best see Mr. Riggs about it. He'll be in by nine in the morning, I expect."

"I'm not a salesman." Richard pocketed the key and moved a little distance across the lobby to get a paper.

There was silence, and Richard stole another glance at the man behind the desk. The pudgy night clerk gave a shrug. "Well, if you've a mind to visit Rena tonight, I wouldn't. She's, well, indisposed—not been feeling too well of late, you might say." He seemed pleased with his disposition of the matter. "Perhaps you'd like to see Miss Kremser. She's the woman who lives with her."

At the mention of Lenore Kremser's name, Richard's jaw tightened. He took a long breath and attempted to smile. "Thanks."

He let himself out, glad for the wash of fragrant air. Following the desk clerk's directions, he found cabin 7 and dropped his valise and two-suiter by the door. The cabin, although clean and suitably furnished, struck him as tawdry and stuffy. Something repugnant settled around him that he feared had nothing at all to do with the cabin; he thrust the windows open, letting the cool wind from the lake soothe his uneasiness, and unpacked his suitcase.

He had avoided driving too near to the stone mansion. Time enough for that tomorrow, he reasoned. For tonight he would try to rest and decide how to proceed with the purpose of this trip. He felt a shiver race through him. Such an eerie quiet clung to this place.

His things arranged, Richard put on a plaid shirt and tucked it inside his gray slacks. He put on a pair of boots, locked the cabin, and walked out to look around. The sun had slipped behind the bluff, and only the barest trace of pink light glowed from behind the hills. He walked along the road, watching lights come on in cabin windows. A few hardy vacationers still sat outside cabins on lawn chairs, but most had gone inside, fleeing the advancing night chill.

Richard walked on, watching the stars appear and listening to the gurgling sounds from the lake. Could it really be true that his mother had owned this place for ten years and he was only now experiencing his first visit? *Mother*. The word, even though unspoken, seemed strange in his mind. Even as a boy, he had called her Rena, not Mother. Rena had liked it that way.

Perhaps it wasn't her fault, he thought. Just giving birth to a baby doesn't make a woman a mother. For Rena the role never quite fit. And it had taken him a long time to get over the sense of being an accident, an intrusion on the life and space of another.

Rena's marriage to Richard's father had been a marriage for profit. Rena needed to be successful, to be surrounded by symbols of success. And Father loved Rena, so much that he was willing to put up with her incessant, and sometimes ruthless, push to the top. Richard recalled frequent, demoralizing arguments over money.

He threw a pebble into the lake, watched the ripples circle, widen, and disappear in watery oblivion. The best schools, the proper clothes, the trips, none of them had satisfied the real needs of a boy. He remembered growing up feeling like the pebble now being swept away into meaninglessness.

When his father had died of a massive heart attack, Richard had packed his things, withdrawn the sizable savings that had accrued to him, and had left the suburban ranch-style house. Funny, he couldn't remember anything about that house except the sprawling outline of it, bleak and dark on cold autumn days.

"You hate me, don't you?" Rena had pouted, a cocktail glass in her slender fingers. Her strawberry blond hair had become dislodged from its careful coiffure, and a lock dropped fretfully over her left eye.

He hadn't said anything. If he had, he might have cried. A seventeen-year-old boy shouldn't be found crying in the presence of his mother, especially when he was determined never to see her again. Maybe he had hated her. He knew that he had hated the parties, the drinking, the currying favor of rich friends, the loneliness, the desperate loneliness.

"Goodbye, Rena," he had said huskily as he walked out the door. Now, fifteen years later, he had achieved a measure of success himself. He owned a sizable advertising agency in Minneapolis, and he enjoyed the respect of his fellows, the satisfaction of hard work, and the things that money could buy. When Susanna came along, he felt as if he might have been born under some lucky star after all.

He'd invited Rena to the wedding. Perhaps she couldn't forgive him for walking out after Dad's death. Maybe she just hadn't wanted to be bothered. For whatever reason, she hadn't come. It was no blow to him. Undoubtedly she had been involved in another grandiose business venture. But family members had hinted that Rena was in trouble. Her heavy drinking was taking its toll on her health and her finances. It occurred to Richard that Rena's wealth had to be markedly more substantial than even he had known to stand the cost of her lifestyle.

There had been little time to worry about his mother's health. His own business had demanded much of him and his marriage. Susanna had become dissatisfied, restless. Perhaps if they had had children, things would have changed. No, he was grateful they hadn't, even more grateful as Susanna had begun to assuage her unhappiness with liquor. He could remember the horror of the first time he had come home and found her passed out in their living room.

He had cut his business appointments down to dangerous levels, had spent hours with her in beautiful resorts, had bought her gifts, had provided expensive counseling, but had seen none of these things effecting any sort of change. Susanna wanted out of the marriage, and no amount of pleading and changing on his part made the least bit of difference.

One cold Friday he had come home early from a business appointment and had found Susanna in the bedroom with a man from their travel bureau. It was enough. After two years of marriage, he gave her the divorce she wanted.

Richard turned back toward his cabin, feeling a coldness in him that had little to do with the brisk night air. Something in him had died that Friday five years ago. His sense of failure settled deep in him, and yet, he was too analytical, too intelligent not to see that his failure was echoed in countless others.

Few of his business associates had succeeded in matters of family and personal integrity. He had seen that one could orbit space, turn deserts into agricultural centers, amass great sums of money, accomplish revolutionary medical miracles, but could not build positive human relationships.

Somewhere in the course of those five years since his divorce, Richard began to realize the absolute poverty of humanity. What was there of goodness, of purity, of truth in the whole world? Surely only God Himself—and He must be there if there was any sense to anything—could make anything worthy of the mess of his life. Totally ignorant of the ways of religion or the Bible, Richard nonetheless set out to find God. His mistakes over the years stung him with incredible remorse.

"You hate me, don't you?" His mother's words those many years before came flooding back.

He had simply said goodbye, never challenging the statement. Now, after several attempts to talk with her, letters, and cards on her birthday, he had found the courage to face her.

He knew that Rena's business was suffering, although as he looked around the property and its full complement of guests, he could not understand why. Why were thousands of dollars being lost annually from the business profits? He had written to Rena about this, offered several times to help in the past five years. But Rena wouldn't listen. Why? Did she hate him that much? Did she think he wanted her money? Why wouldn't she listen?

Richard found his way back to the cabin, unlaced his boots, and stretched out on the bed. He must find some way to help. Had the alcohol so muddled Rena's mind? She once had had such a good mind. She could turn a profit like no one else he'd ever known. Well, at least she'd passed that on to him. His own business savvy was extraordinary, people said. Amazing what satisfaction there was in that, until you began to see all that was really precious in life fall apart and leave you alone to the emptiness of yourself.

What was it that the Scriptures said? "What shall it profit a man if he gain the whole world and lose his own soul?" He had only begun to understand what that meant.

In his seeking he had found much that was confusing, even disappointing, but something told him he was going in the right direction. The direction seemed to take him to his mother. Somehow she was all tied up with his own search for meaning and peace.

The lake loons lulled him, and finally he gave up the confusing images, the regrets of the past, the concerns over the future that hovered dizzily in his mind. He slept well but woke just as the sun was coming up, and it seemed he'd been asleep only moments.

Nevertheless, he showered and dressed in boots and a fleece-lined jacked and set out toward the wooded bluff where Rena lived. Just why he was going there now he couldn't be sure. It would be hours before Rena would be awake, hours before he could decently call on her. Perhaps he wanted to get a look at the house, get some feeling about the place first.

He reveled in the damp soundness of earth under his feet and the fragrance of the unspoiled day. Ahead rose the forested area along the misty bluff that would lead eventually to the house. He had marked it well from the road the evening before. It couldn't be seen from the usually traversed vacation area; in fact, he doubted if anyone knew that the stone house had any relation to the resort below.

He passed the beach, the sprawling golf course, and followed on as the road ended and a small trail rose through a pine forest. The morning hush struck him like some magic spell, so that his own footfall seemed a wanton violence as he stepped cautiously over the needle-strewn ground. It was as though Nature had freshly scrubbed the carpet and would scold him for making spots on it. He moved lush foliage aside and climbed higher on the bluff until suddenly the brush and evergreens gave way to an open plain.

The house towered over the landscape like a gray monster, its many "eyes" keeping watch in a kind of smoky belligerence. A neatly rolled black roof, like hair carefully groomed into a pageboy, curled over the gray edges. An old-fashioned turret rose like a medieval black hat. This elegant, carefully restored turn-of-the-century home would have captured Rena's interest and been enough to demand her energies. It was like her to choose this site to plan her vacation resort.

He sat under a spreading tree and wondered about the woman inside the formidable house. Once he had been determined never to see her again. Now fear or awe or a mixture of both clung to him as he pictured her. What would she be like now? Would she see him or turn him away?

The sun rose higher in the expanse of sky and Richard crept away from his semihiding place. But who was to see him here? he wondered. No one came near here. And Rena was never one to rise early. Besides, folks could take the road to the private drive that led to her house if they chose to visit. There was no need to take the shortcut through the woods.

The loneliness, the sense of abandonment, the wounds ached in him, but he must not let them conquer him. He lifted his face to the warming sun, wishing he knew the words for a real prayer. Then he slipped back into the forest and climbed down into the lush depths, glad for the sweet envelopment of it, the kindly shelter of it.

Suddenly he was arrested by the sound of singing: a clear-toned lyrical soprano melody more beautiful than anything he had heard before seemed a part of the heady aroma of pine and the spangled sun rays shooting through the foliage. He stopped still, listening to a woman's voice in a kind of primal, yearning song.

He moved down a little and pulled back a sweep of branches. And there he saw her, her hands poised on the trunk of a birch tree, her face raised up to a vacant space where the dome of heaven looked in with a shine of gold.

Her hair shimmered like a wreath of light about the oval of her face. Her brown eyes with a tender glowing made him hold his breath. She wore a pale blue sweater that gave her a delicate, angelic look. Perhaps he was still sleeping. Perhaps the woods had cast some spell over him.

She moved from the tree and, turning, held her arms up to grasp an overhanging branch. The opalescent light outlined the smooth curve of her figure. Richard felt a tender yearning come over him, such as he recalled the first time he had watched the sun die crimson with its pain on the black arms of the ocean.

Suddenly the twig in his fingers snapped. The incredible singing stopped. He let the branches fall back in place before she had time to whirl around and soundlessly crept away down the wooded glen, breaking a new trail. But the beauty of her face lingered over him long after he'd returned to his cabin.

four

> Music, when soft voices die,
> Vibrates in the memory—
> Odours, when sweet violets sicken,
> Live within the sense they quicken.
>
> PERCY BYSSHE SHELLEY

Angie stepped back to get a good look at her painting. With a critical eye she scrutinized the blue lake, the tiny white-gold diamonds sprinkled on the horizon, and the sailboat dipping, dancing at dawn, its white sails gleaming against a panorama of pink and yellow streamers. Here and there the ribbons turned crimson and golden like heralding banners.

She frowned, dissatisfied with her rendition, and looked away at the real scene, pondering Nature's timeless beauty. It was ancient beauty, and yet it could strike the heart dead center as though one were seeing it for the very first time.

She had set up her easel on the hill above the row of cabins where she could look down and see the blue expanse of water. Around her butterflies and morning insects busied themselves, and the hours quickly passed. Now she could tell by the nearly overhead position of the sun that she had painted the morning away, but painting had not brought the consolation that she needed. The heaviness of her spirit seemed to set her apart from her surroundings, and she felt detached, alone.

She folded up the aluminum legs and strapped them into place on the easel, put the palette and brushes inside the canvas flap on the portable rig, and started back down the hill. Jen had been gone only a day. She missed her already.

When she had lugged all the painting materials back to the cabin, Angie changed into slacks and a loose cotton shirt. She belted the shirt around her waist, slipped into her sandals, and threw some change and a comb into a denim purse. Maybe she would go down to the beach and buy one of those long hot dogs smothered with mustard. It would be fun to take a long walk or to sit in the cove of rocks and watch the people and the rhythm of life.

Do me a favor, and look in on Aunt Rena. Jen's request came suddenly to mind. *She ought to be told about my father.*

Angie hadn't forgotten. She'd have a hot dog and climb up to the stone house, using her familiar wooded path. Sudden anxiety tingled in her stomach as she thought of the foreboding house she had come upon; was it only yesterday? The sound of breaking branches, the eerie sense of being observed . . . these came clouding her mind. Perhaps she should take the road instead.

I hate to ask you. I hope my aunt won't be rude, Jen had said. She had seemed particularly worried about her aunt's behavior.

Rudeness from people was hardly a cause for concern. Angie had endured the worst of antagonisms. But there was something else. Was it the fear of failure? Her caring had not been enough to help Eddie and the others. She scolded herself. Rena was a lonely woman to whom she could extend a friendly word, a kindness, perhaps.

Impulsively Angie picked up the little ceramic music box from her dresser. It wasn't really a box, but a figurine of a woman holding a small child on her lap. The woman's left hand held an open book from which she might have been reading to the pale-haired child who looked up into the mother's face with delight.

Angie flipped the silver latch. "Jesus loves me, this I know, for the Bible tells me so," the tinkling music played.

She had no flowers to bring to this woman who had not been well; perhaps she would like the music box. Angie had bought it only a month ago, and it still shone with newness. She put a bit of tissue around the figurine and dropped it into her denim purse.

The beach was alive with people, some moving about, others stretched out in the sun. Children ran and skipped. One licked a cherry Popsicle that dripped in a long stream, making red rivulets on her arms and bare stomach. A young couple enmeshed in each other's tanned arms lay on a strip of towel, so that they seemed to be one brown body with too many arms and legs.

Farther back from the shore elderly couples with umbrellas over their heads read books and newspapers as they reclined on long chaise lounges. Angie bought a hot dog and sat down on a little cluster of rocks near the refreshment bar. She loved to watch the people, to wonder who they were, what they thought about. As a child she used to make up stories about them. Round and round they'd twirl in her head: noble characters, evil ones, sad ones, energetic ones, kind ones.

Her hot dog consumed, Angie set off on her errand, sensing a certain hesitancy. The road to the stone mansion was hedged by tall birches, overspreading weeds, and scrub pine that never grew to height. Narrow and steep it wound, and it seemed a long way from the edge of the resort to the peak on which the house stood.

Even in the afternoon sunshine the house loomed from shadow, ominous and forbidding. No flowers bloomed to interrupt its somber, gray facade. Massive stone pillars framed the entrance at the end of a winding driveway, and the three oaks in the front yard seemed a part of it, rising in oneness with the pillars.

Hardly had she set foot on the wide veranda when two great dogs the color of gray stone leaped from behind the structure, barking and bearing down on her with raised hackles, eyes glowing like heated coals, and mouths gaping with spiny teeth. She froze, expecting to experience the hot bloody grip of their jaws, when abruptly they halted with a choking cry. Only then did she see the long silver chains attached to their collars.

She clung to the pillar, giddy with relief. Suddenly the door swung open. She saw a woman, tall and reedlike in a fashionable suit the color of charcoal and a gray striped blouse that rose in a high ruffle about her neck. Her hair was black, so black that it nearly lost all color in the shine of the sun upon it.

"Honcho! Jack! Quiet!" she called. Her flawlessly succinct reprimand sent the dogs shrinking back, their tails drooping behind them. But her level, green-eyed gaze never left Angie's face. "May I help you?" she asked, stepping out onto the porch.

Angie stepped away from the pillar and readjusted the strap of her purse. The marvelous green eyes compelled her. "I—I came to see Mrs. Mara. I have a message for her from her niece." Her own voice sounded small, distant. She cleared her throat and met the cool, intrusive gaze.

Suddenly the woman's manner changed. She flashed an ingratiating smile that transformed her. "Oh, I see. Miss . . . Miss . . ."

"Carlson, Angie Carlson. I was vacationing with Jennifer Flurry, Mrs. Mara's niece."

"Yes, of course. Please come in." She extended a slender, ringless hand with meticulously manicured nails. "I'm terribly sorry if the dogs frightened you. Mrs. Mara is very insistent about her privacy and we have had some difficulty with prowlers of late. You understand."

The woman, probably in her early thirties, ushered Angie into a large room, sparsely but elegantly furnished. A reupholstered Victorian couch with clawlike feet graced the long wall in front of sweeping velvet drapes of pale blue. On an adjoining wall stood an upright piano from which two brass candlesticks rose like periscopes from a gleaming black sea.

Angie's feet sank into the sculptured blue and gold carpet as she followed the woman into the room. This was undoubtedly the personal secretary that Jen had mentioned.

"I'm Lenore Kremser, Rena Mara's personal . . . secretary." She seemed uncomfortable with the term but quickly recovered. "I hope you'll not be too disappointed, but Mrs. Mara rarely receives guests. She's not been too well. . . ."

Angie waited for the rest of the sentence, but it was obvious that Lenore Kremser was not prepared to say more. "I'm terribly sorry. I hope it isn't too serious," Angie said. She recalled Jen's words about Rena's alcoholism. "Perhaps some company will cheer her," Angie continued. "I promised Jen that I would come."

"I must consider Rena's wishes. I agree that it would be better for Mrs. Mara to get out more, to see people more frequently, but I am bound to carry out her wishes."

Angie unzipped her purse. At least she could leave the little gift with Lenore. "Will you please tell her that Jennifer's father has had a heart attack. Jen has gone to be with him. I'm certain Mrs. Mara would want to know."

"How dreadful," Lenore said, knitting her brows together in one black line. "I'm very sorry. How kind of you to come and let us know. I'll certainly tell her." Lenore paused at the spiral staircase near the door as though waiting for Angie to take her leave.

Angie regarded her closely, aware of something too coldly professional, too polite and businesslike. And yet. . . . Aloud she said, "I understand that Jen's mother and Mrs. Mara are sisters."

"Yes. I have occasionally helped Rena with her correspondence with her sister. I'm sure that she'll be grateful for your information. Now, if you'll excuse me—"

"What is it, Lenore?" A husky, curiously petulant voice came from the top of the spiral staircase.

Rena Ogden Mara, a full-breasted woman with an amazingly slim waistline, stood on the landing, her pale aqua dressing gown draping the top step. Her fading red hair, softened by even streaks of silver, waved into a knot at the top of her head, giving the allusion of height. A stray lock of hair dipped over her left eye, rendering her handsome features curiously childlike.

"Oh, Rena, I'm sorry to disturb you." Lenore Kremser hurried up the staircase with quick agility and swept a charcoal-suited arm around the older woman's waist.

"Here, let's get you back to bed."

"Just a moment." Something reminiscent of an air of command colored the woman's voice. Then quickly, the vulnerable softness returned. "Do I know you, young lady?"

Angie took a few steps up the stairs.

Lenore broke in quickly. "Rena, this is Angie Carlson. She's a friend of Miss Flurry's, your niece. I told her that you weren't feeling well right now. Perhaps she can return at a more convenient time—"

"Please, Lenore. Ask her to come in. I'm feeling quite well enough."

Lenore was momentarily speechless. She led Rena to the bed inside a spacious, shade-drawn room.

"Lenore, please draw back the drapes. It's dark in here."

Angie took a chair near the bed and waited while Lenore opened the heavy curtains. Light spilled in, revealing a soft mauve carpet and an old-fashioned drop-front desk.

Lenore paused by the opposite side of Rena's bed as if she expected to be part of the visit.

"Thank you, Lenore." It was a dismissal.

"Are you certain?"

"Quite. Thank you, Lenore."

She left, discontent glowered in her green eyes. Was there a toss, ever so slight, of the regal head? wondered Angie.

Angie turned her attention to her dubious hostess. Rena Mara's eyes, a pale blue as though they had faded from many washings of tears, met hers.

"I prefer to entertain my guests in the sitting room. Ah,

but the years have not been kind. You say you're a friend of Jennifer's? Please, tell me your message." There was no hint of anxiety in the request, but a weary apprehension, as if she had long ago steeled herself for the worst.

"Jen would have come herself. She—we—are grateful for your kindness in offering us a cabin here. This is such a lovely place. We came only two days ago, and yesterday Jen received a phone call. Her father has suffered a heart attack. Jen has gone to be with him and your sister."

Rena sighed. "Jennifer was always such a good girl, perhaps better than John and Beth deserved. Poor John."

She stopped and tucked the stray lock of hair back in place. Angie noticed the pale white circles on Rena's small hand where at least two rings had left their imprints.

"I'm afraid I've not done too well by my family. You see, I've always been a . . . career woman . . . kept very busy. It's been a long time since I've seen either of them, or Jennifer."

Angie watched the pale eyes drift past her and beyond to the window where a tree branch scraped softly against a screen. The sound of it was like a gentle sigh.

"Jennifer—I hope she is well?" Without waiting for an answer she added, "I've never had . . . a daughter."

"What about your son, Mrs. Mara?" Angie asked quietly, remembering what Jen had said about a young man named Rick with whom she had played as a child.

The soft lips turned suddenly thin and taut, and the little blue veins in her neck twitched. Her eyes, startled at first, took on an austere remoteness. Then there came a little joyless laugh.

"Yes, I had a son. One day seventeen years ago he said goodbye. I'd almost forgotten about him," she finished bitterly. Rena stared out the far window.

"I'm sorry," Angie whispered.

Quickly her mood changed. "How dreadful of me not to offer you some refreshment. Perhaps I have something here," Rena said as she made a move toward the cabinet next to her bed.

"Please, don't trouble yourself. I've just eaten lunch. I don't care for anything." Angie stared at the liquor cabinet, ominously well stocked.

Rena lay back against a plump pillow.

"Mrs. Mara," Angie said, opening her denim purse, "I brought you something. I hope you don't mind. But Jen said you hadn't been feeling well." She drew the tissue-wrapped music box from her purse. "I thought this might please you." She held it out to Rena.

"A present?" Rena looked curiously into Angie's face. She took the little package and opened it with clumsy fingers. The lock of hair fell once again over her left eye. She let the wrappings fall and held the box in both hands. She gently caressed the figurine as if she were a blind woman. Then, finding the little switch, she pressed it with one finger.

The soft strains of "Jesus Loves Me" filled the room. It played until it wound itself down to silence. Still Rena did not speak.

Angie watched the pulsing of the little veins in Rena's neck and the almost imperceptible trembling of her lips. Then abruptly Rena placed the music box on the dresser.

"Thank you," the woman said in a small voice, her eyes averted. "I'm tired now. . . ."

Angie rose, slipping the strap of her purse over her shoulder. Perhaps it had been a foolish gift, inappropriate at best. She turned and walked heavily to the door.

"Miss Carlson—"

"Please, call me Angie."

"I . . ." Rena took a deep breath, then turned her filmy eyes on Angie. Something in her look struck at Angie's heart, as though all the loneliness of the whole world were mirrored there. In Rena's face she read the same longings, the same hungers, that she had come to know in Eddie's sister Roslyn and the others, and in Eddie . . . before. She swallowed and waited, not knowing what to say.

"If you've nothing to do, some time that is, will you come to see me again?"

Angie smiled. "Of course." She wanted to rush to Rena, to hold the white hand against the aqua gown, but she did not. "I promise," she whispered softly and left the bedroom.

five

> The thing we long for, that we are
> For one transcendent moment,
> Before the Present poor and bare
> Can make its sneering comment.
>
> JAMES RUSSELL LOWELL

She stood on a grassy knoll in the semidarkness. Willows, cloaking her shoulders with long, spiny leaves, rubbed their damp blades against her bare arms until she felt chilled to the bone. It grew darker, and the darker it became the farther she could see into the velvet landscape beyond, stretching like dark green theater curtains, flowing and curving into mysterious shapes and rhythms.

Beyond the cloistered spot where she waited, unable to draw herself away from the willows' hold, a long pathway wound its way to the precipice of a great ravine. How is it that she could see so clearly in this deepening night? But no, it wasn't night, not really.

Suddenly a butterfly, more enormous and beautiful than any she had ever seen, appeared. Carmine red with glittering silver wings and horrible antennae, it shimmered crimson in the translucent blackness. It fluttered in a crazy zigzag pattern, as though beckoning Angie to follow, but she couldn't move. She struggled against the force of the slimy foliage, but she was powerless to move even a finger.

As she watched in terror a figure appeared. He was chasing the butterfly, running this way and that, jumping with outstretched arms. There was something strange about that figure, thought Angie. Pencil-thin legs and great floppy shoes, ears that stuck out from straw-colored hair. Eddie! It was Eddie. But what was Eddie doing here? Angie squinted in the shadows.

Suddenly behind him came another figure, then another. Eddie. Another just like Eddie! A stream of little boys, each a copy of Eddie, chased the giant insect. They were headed for the ravine. Then behind Eddie came an undulating female form. The girl's eyes were fastened on the enormous insect. Her lips parted in a rapturous smile that cracked and fell away in one horrid moment. She was Roslyn, Eddie's older sister, protector, surrogate mother, but still a child.

Angie screamed. But no sound came. Over and over she struggled and screamed her silent screams that no one could hear. And the butterfly flew crazily on its laughing wings. She watched Eddie stumble over the edge of the precipice, his childish yell piercing her heart. And each little Eddie in turn fell domino-style over the edge in a continuous screaming echo. Roslyn was at the brink now, her body twisted with terror. Soon she would fall into the abyss.

And suddenly Angie awoke, trembling and cold. She lay in the strange bed, relieved that what she had just experienced was a crazy, inexplicable dream, a nightmare. From her window, the tall pine bluff rose bluish green, a faint morning mist clustering over it. She was viewing Pinewood Lake as calm as a gallery pastoral, in shocking contrast to her frightening dream.

She hadn't had a nightmare since her childhood, at least not one that she could remember. She drew herself up against the headboard of the bed, fixing her eyes hungrily on the pastel serenity of the landscape from her window. Although relieved that the nightmare wasn't real, the catalyst for the dream had been very real indeed. Eddie, a poor, lost child too good for this world, had been the victim of the great silver butterfly. Perhaps Roslyn would be next.

Roslyn, fifteen, surrogate mother, vulnerable child in a woman's body . . . What would happen to her? Angie had tried to befriend her, but the reaction had always been the same. Roslyn didn't want to talk to or trust anyone. Angie recalled her now as she had seen her, in black lace gauntlet gloves that began at her knuckles and reached clear to her armpits like some kind of medieval costume. A magenta dress flounced high above her shapely knees, and her supple, voluptuous body swayed almost imperceptibly, as though to some unplayed rhythm. Great rubbery bracelets hung from her wrists and left ankle; bangles and beads clung to the bareness of her chest. Wild dark hair frizzed to her shoulders. Somewhere in its maze was a gauzy rag of purple and yellow, reminiscent of a current rock singer. Roslyn's eyes, heavy with mascara and at the same time demurely shy, always averted direct contact.

When Roslyn had come to the mission that horrible Thursday, she had spoken with a voice whispery with fear and dread. For all her hard exterior, there was a tenderness about her where Eddie was concerned. But Eddie was missing, and she was frantic. Her large eyes, smudged and dripping mascara, had pleaded for help.

The police had later found Eddie in the abandoned warehouse where he often went to play and to sneak up on the older boys and discover their secrets. He had been lying in a fetal position, as though he had just curled up to return to that earlier existence where life was warm and kind. He had been strangled. A child of sixteen, notorious in the neighborhood for assorted grievances against society, had ended Eddie's poor little life.

They had all grieved. Mrs. Packett had provided a special supper for the family members who gathered in the tawdry upstairs apartment to sit with Sandra Loss. Only Eddie's mission friends had come to watch his small body lowered into the ground. Death happened on a daily basis there in the bowels of the city. But Angie hadn't fully realized until now how she had loved this little child. Something in her had broken too. She had been unable to save him. What was the use of it all?

Maybe death was an accepted thing in the inner city, like drugs, poverty, and crime. These always led to despair and death. But Eddie shouldn't have had to pay. He was only a child, an innocent child.

She got up and paced the floor of the cabin, glad for the coldness beneath her feet, solid coldness. Perhaps there would be a message from Jen today. She put on her jeans and a sweatshirt and brewed the coffee a little stronger than usual.

When nine o'clock came, Angie walked toward the resort office. She'd see if a letter had come, then take a ride into the little town and check out the shops. There was nothing like a good dose of shopping to make her forget her troubles.

The morning sun warmed her back as she walked along the little path toward the office, and blades of grass sparkled like silver knives on a well-laid table. The cloth was the color of emeralds, and white daisies with yellow centers made up the floral pattern. There was a domesticity about it, a warmth that flooded her heart and set her remembering again.

She wondered now what her life would have been like if she had married Rob. She hadn't been ready then. Something deep and strong strove within her, something she had to do. Rob hadn't understood. Neither had she really. So it had ended. Rob had moved on to a stable job and had married a woman with platinum hair and a taste for poodles; Angie had begun her work among the people of the inner city where poodles had no place in the day-to-day rush of life.

She walked on, willing the memories away. The mingled fragrance of marigolds and petunias heralded her fast approach to the gleaming glass doors of the resort office. As she came back to reality she saw a man approaching from the opposite end of the walk that led from the parking lot.

Attaché case in hand and pin-striped suit perfectly complemented by white shirt and maroon tie, the man moved with an athletic gait. He was of medium height with very broad shoulders and a thick neck, probably a football player in college. He had arrived at the door first and stood holding it for her, a wide smile on his somewhat ruddy face.

"Good morning," he said with a slight bow. He arched copper-colored brows, a steady, if not bold, interest sparking his eyes. They were blue, but not like the blue of water. Touches of slate darkened them, so that they were more like the sky just beginning to darken before a storm. Little steely edges rimmed their dark circles.

"Oh, good morning," Angie said. She stepped inside,

aware of the man's aftershave lotion, which vied for prominence over the marigolds and petunias they passed.

"It's a great morning," the man said as he followed her in, those dark blue eyes commanding her attention. "Can I be of service perhaps?"

Angie looked up, surprised.

"I'm the manager here," he said, setting his briefcase down at his feet and extending a large hand on which reddish hairs shone in the gleam of the sun through the window. "Harrington Riggs," he said. "I hope you're enjoying Pinewood Acres."

"Oh, yes. I've only been here a few days, but everything's perfect." She withdrew her hand, which he seemed in no hurry to release. "I'm Angie Carlson. You perhaps know my friend Jennifer Flurry. Her aunt owns this resort."

"Really." Harrington Riggs narrowed his eyes in obvious surprise. "I'm afraid that I haven't met your friend."

Angie looked away uncomfortably. There was something intrusive about those deep blue eyes. "Actually I was hoping for a message from her. You see, she was called away our first night here by her family. Her father's had a heart attack." She felt suddenly desolate and was surprised by the catch in her voice. Tears came too easily these days.

"Oh, I'm sorry. A bummer of a thing to happen on your vacation." His voice grew gentle, and a sympathetic indulgence softened the look in his eye. "Look, come into my office. Tinker will have coffee going. I'll see if there have been any messages for you and be right in."

"Oh, no. I can check myself—"

"Now don't argue." He placed a warm hand on her shoulder and turned her in the direction of the office. "We cater to our customers here," he said with a wink. "Do you take sugar?"

"No," she answered meekly. She went obediently into his office and sat down, suddenly glad for a friendly voice and a chance to relate the things that had happened since coming to the resort.

Harrington Riggs returned quickly with two cups of steaming coffee. "I'm sorry, but there were no messages or mail for you today," he said as he settled himself into his desk chair.

He had removed his suit coat, and now his white shirt stretched tightly across the expanse of his chest. The blue-stoned cuff links that he adjusted spoke of a rather elegant taste. This was a man who liked to live well. Somehow it didn't seem to fit with his build, which was more cotton-knit sweaters and slacks.

"Is everything satisfactory in your cabin, Miss—?" He paused and quickly attempted to ingratiate himself. "You said it was Angie, didn't you?"

She nodded, strangely glad to hear her name spoken, even though something in his manner made her hesitate.

"Yes," he continued, "Angie it is, and if you call me anything but Harry, I'll have to double your rent." He sipped his coffee and watched her over the rim of the cup. "Your first visit here?"

"Yes. Jennifer—my friend—invited me. As I said, her aunt is Mrs. Mara. I met the lady yesterday."

Harry leaned forward slightly in his chair, cup poised in midair. "Oh?" He set the cup down and leaned back deliberately.

Angie quickly relived the tension of that first encounter, the startling introduction by Honcho and Jack, as

Lenore Kremser had called them. "Jennifer wanted me to inform her aunt about her father's heart attack. Mrs. Mara and Jennifer's mother are sisters."

"I see." Harry drew in his lower lip with his teeth and traced the rim of his cup with a thick forefinger. "And how did you find our Mrs. Mara?"

The question had a patronizing sound, but he quickly flashed his broad smile. "I trust she appreciated the efforts of such a lovely young lady."

Angie dropped her eyes, suddenly feeling nervous and ill at ease. Quickly she recovered herself. "How long has she been this way, Mr. Riggs?" she asked.

"It's Harry, remember? Be careful or I'll have Lenore doctor your bill!" Abruptly his smile relaxed and he gave a rather exaggerated sigh. "I'm afraid Mrs. Mara rather enjoys her bottle, but who am I to judge? I do my job and try not to ask questions."

Angie recalled Jen's comments about the resort's problems and the dwindling resources, and she wanted to ask about it. But Mr. Harrington Riggs seemed disinclined to discuss business. "Now, my dear, tell me about yourself."

Strange, that manner of his, as though she were a child and not only slightly younger than him, she thought. Yet in her loneliness she didn't find this irritating. It was nice to have someone strong befriending her. "Not much to tell," she responded. "I'm just a working girl on a holiday, enjoying the comforts of this very pleasant place." She rose and set her cup on Harry's desk. She had no intention of discussing her occupation with him. The very idea seemed ludicrous, and there was a certain comfort in anonymity.

"Must you go so soon?" he asked, rising.

"I'm going into town to do a little shopping. I promised Mrs. Mara I'd come see her again, too," Angie said, adjusting her purse strap.

There was a brief silence, and Angie was surprised to see Harry's concern and studied frown. Looking up, Harry flashed his brilliant smile.

"On a beautiful day like this, with all the entertainment offered at Pinewood Acres, you'd spend your time with an old, befuddled widow like—" He broke off, perhaps noting something in Angie's manner. "That is, I'd think you would want to spend your time swimming and sunning and—"

Angie crossed the room toward the door, glancing back over her shoulder with an amused smile on her face, enjoying his incredulity and at the same time wondering at the sudden tension her words had caused. Was there some reason he didn't want her to visit Mrs. Mara?

"I'll be doing plenty of sunning and swimming, I'm sure, Mr. Riggs . . . Harry. And thank you for the coffee." She was genuinely grateful for his attention, for she felt suddenly less isolated, more encouraged about the prospects of the day. She had been lonely here, she realized, really lonely.

"Remember, if there's anything I can do to make your visit with us more comfortable, please don't hesitate to ask." The professional sounding words didn't quite match his scrutinizing look or his indulgent hand on her shoulder.

These she ignored and went to the bus stop, wondering about Rena Mara, about the coldly efficient Lenore Kremser, and about the enigmatic Mr. Riggs whom she felt might easily have made a pass at her had she been inclined to encourage him.

six

> If I should meet thee
> After long years,
> How should I greet thee? —
> With silence and tears.
>
> LORD BYRON

Rena felt herself being propelled up the long driveway to the stone mansion. She smoothed the waves of her hair and tucked in the loose tendrils at the back of her neck. She checked the buttons of her jade silk dress with fingers not quite willing to obey.

Was it dark already? She hadn't meant to stay so long. Well, if she was lucky she could make it up to her room before Lenore saw her. She didn't want to see the veiled disgust in those cool eyes. There would be no open censure. Indeed, a sweet, consoling smile would part those perfect lips. She would scold her too fondly and help her to bed. Just once she wished that Lenore would come out with it, call her a ——. Rena drew in a sharp breath that caught in her throat like a sob.

The car door opened. A draft of air cooled her flushed face. She grasped the handles of her purse and drew herself slowly out.

"Here, let's give you an arm, Ms. Mara." The night desk clerk who had brought her home held out a pudgy hand.

A little circle of light from the yard lamp shone on his bald head, making it appear yellow. The smell of pine cleaner and stale cigarette smoke clung to his baggy clothes and trailed after him in a dubious aura. She had probably interrupted his cleaning chores when she had phoned for a ride, she realized. He had a condescending air of one who felt her his equal but who had no right to say so.

"Never mind, Tinker. I can walk. I'm not an invalid," she said with a sharpness that surprised herself. She stood up and fought the reeling dizziness in her head.

"If you don't mind my saying so, madam, you've had a mite too much to drink." He seemed delighted with his proclamation and rocked a little back and forth on his heels, his hands stuck in the pockets of his rumpled pants.

Rena steadied herself on the opened car door and drew herself up to her full height so that her eyes bore into those of the squat man. "I'm quite capable of deciding for myself, and of getting into my own house." She hoped that the deliberateness of her statement, brought on by her anger, overcame the slurring speech.

The little man shrugged and moved off, twitching his nose as though he had an itch he couldn't scratch.

With a noble effort Rena climbed the three steps onto the porch and let herself in with the key she had wisely placed in the pocket of her dress. Did she still have her purse? Well, no matter.

Honcho and Jack strained on their chains, their eyes watchful, with a kind of glazed acceptance in them. Why did Lenore tolerate those beasts? "Trespassers," Lenore had said. Well, if there were trespassers around, she hadn't seen any, Rena decided.

Inside the foyer she leaned against the door, listening. She could hear Tinker's car lumbering back down the drive a little too fast. Soon its smoldering died into a faint hum like that from a drowsy mosquito, and she was blissfully alone.

She dropped down onto the Victorian couch and ran her hand appreciatively over its contoured arm. Surprisingly she found herself taken back in time and hearing again the refined Irish tones of her father's voice.

"Ah, you've an eye for the fine things in life, Rena. To win them you'll have to work hard, to fight for what you want. No one's going to be giving you a handout, my lady. What you want you must take. And don't be apologizing to any man."

She trembled as she remembered. It was as though she were seventeen again, her long red hair falling on soft shoulders, her blue eyes eager, her mind mesmerized by his words and by the confident gleam in his eyes. Oh, she would make him proud of her, very proud. Maybe then he would love her.

Had he loved Mama? Rena tried to sort it out in the fogginess of her mind, which whirled with images gradually becoming clear like when wind settles and no longer troubles the water. It had been so long ago. Still she could see a picture of a stunningly beautiful woman with sad eyes of no particular color and every color, eyes from whose depths tears were natural companions. Whenever Papa was gone she would hum strange, haunting melodies.

One day the songs had ended. The beautiful lady was gone. And Rena had often cried because she could not remember her or even the way her arms around her might have felt. She had been little more than a baby when Mother died.

Papa had never remarried, but he had employed an endless stream of nannies to care for Rena and her younger sister Beth. Now it was too hard to recall any of those surrogate mothers or to draw forth any feeling other than longing for Papa's next visit, which never came soon enough.

As she had grown, so had her striving for Papa's approval. She had earned high academic awards, excelled in business ventures, and by the time she was seventeen had earned enough money, when added to the business loan Papa had promised, to begin an independent ice-cream store in the small town where they lived. One day, after she had waited for Papa to return from an extended visit in New York, she received the news. He had collapsed in an elevator and died, a victim of a heart attack.

Rena felt the harsh fabric of the couch on her cheek. She should make some coffee. She pulled herself upright, sensing a numbing desolation. She tried to focus on the face of her father, but she could not see him clearly. She wondered vaguely if he would have been proud of her now, if he knew that she was the owner of one of the finest resorts in northern Wisconsin.

The door opened. Lenore Kremser strode in like a flash of sweeping fire. Her black hair curled with an almost unnatural smoothness to the shoulders of her elegant red blouse. The black shininess of her fashionable skirt continued from her waist to midcalf.

Rena raised her eyes to Lenore's face. Why was it so hard to focus on her eyes? Had she had that many drinks?

"Care for a cup of tea?" The precise voice paused, and Lenore gave a scrutinizing glance. "Coffee perhaps?" she suggested.

Lenore looked away but not before Rena had recognized the dreaded look . . . or was it her own stricken conscience that tormented her? Oh, it was all so wearying.

Rena unstrapped her high-heeled shoes and shoved them away with her foot. "Bring me a couple of aspirin. My head hurts," she said.

Lenore walked away to the kitchen and in a moment returned and with a long tapered thrust of her hand extended the water and aspirin.

Rena swallowed them. "What's the count this week, Lenore?"

"We're at our capacity, 112. Every cabin filled." Lenore picked up Rena's shoes and set them on the first step of the spiral staircase.

"That should bring the credit side up quite sig—signif'cantly." Rena felt a glimmer of hope even as she struggled to get her words out right.

"Unfortunately, costs have continued to rise. We'll be lucky to end this season with a profit, once the old bills are paid." Lenore arched a black brow that looked curiously like a sleek black caterpillar.

"I see. Well, I must take a long hard look at things just as soon as I'm . . . on my feet again." Rena's head pounded. She just wanted to lie down.

"You've been away from it for some time. You're not really aware of the costs and the salaries we have to pay these days. Here, drink your coffee. And don't worry. We're going to see this thing turn around soon."

Lenore talked on, as though she wanted to fill all the empty spaces with sound. "I'm glad to see that you're getting out again. Did you have a nice time at the club?"

Did she? Rena wondered. What had possessed her to go there after such a long absence? An oppressive weariness washed over her. "I'm going to bed," she said.

"Certainly. Let me help you."

This time Rena made no effort at independence or dignity. She was too tired. Besides, what did it all matter? What did anything matter? Let the whole world go to——. She felt the room swimming a little, then Lenore's surprisingly strong arm was around her waist, lifting her.

The dogs began to bark, a kind of fretful braying. "What's wrong with those blasted dogs anyway?"

"I'll see to them in just a moment. Let's get you to bed."

The patronizing sweetness in Lenore's voice mocked her. Some long-ago spark in Rena rose, but only for a moment. She was too tired and too sick to protest. Father would understand, wouldn't he?

Lenore was helping her into the aqua dressing gown. Her fingers against Rena's skin were cold, clammy, like the nannies' fingers she recalled from childhood. An enormous pain swept over her.

"I can manage, Lenore." Rena clutched the gown about her for its small warmth and longed for another drink. She could feel Lenore's disapproving eyes. "Leave me alone," she said evenly.

The fretful whining of the dogs grew louder, then fainter as the door at last closed, leaving her alone. She shouldn't even think about the cabinet by her bed, but . . . just one more drink. Maybe then she could sleep. Just one little drink. She wasn't really an . . . was she?

She let her head fall against the pillows and tried not to think about the cabinet. She pulled the pins that bound her hair, feeling only small relief for the ache in her head. She fumbled for a clear spot on the night stand to put the pins, and her hand brushed against something.

Suddenly the high lyric strains of "Jesus Loves Me" sounded in her dulled ear. She clutched the little figurine and put it close to her eyes to see the softly smiling mother and the tender child. She let the music play until it began to die. Then she clicked the silver lever.

Tracing her finger over the smooth lines, she remembered the young woman who had brought the gift. Such a fine face she had, and eyes that had such a clarity, a purity about them. When was it she had come? She had brought some news about Beth.

Rena closed her hand over the music box and thought about her sister. Beth was like their mother had been, weak, fragile, too accepting of whatever fell to her lot. As sisters they had had little in common. Still, Beth had always written a few times a year. Her letters were always solicitous, seldom warm. Nonetheless, they had watched out for each other.

The resort had always been open for Beth and any members of her family. Beth had never come, but for the second time Beth's daughter, Jennifer, was a guest at Pinewood Acres. Rena frowned, trying to remember. Yes, Jennifer had been here, but she had had to leave. Illness . . . her father. Isn't that what the young woman, Angie, had said?

Poor Beth. She had never dealt well with the exigencies of life. She had married John Flurry, strong and sure of himself. He had become her protector, her life. What would Beth do now?

It suddenly occurred to Rena that a very long time had passed since her sister's last letter. Beth had expressed concern over the financial state of Pinewood Acres and had encouraged Rena to seek the aid of Richard, her son, who was also concerned about her situation.

Something nagged at the back of Rena's mind, something about refusing to respond to Richard's letters. But there had been no letters. Surely she couldn't have forgotten that. No, Richard may have told them he had written to his poor old mother, but there had been *no* letters!

A bitter taste rose in her mouth. Richard, her son, concerned? About her? That was a laugh. And if he were concerned now, he undoubtedly was concerned for the money he might—or might not—inherit one day. Suddenly she recalled him as he had been that afternoon so many years before: his tall, slim body framed in the doorway. Behind him summer was dying in a red-gold blaze and leaves from the willow tree in their front yard were falling like crimson tears, some of them weeping on the shining sandy head turned away from her.

"You hate me, don't you?" she had asked.

He had not denied it. Why should he? It was true. He had grown up so soon, before she had had time to know him. But she had had to be gone so much in those early years, hadn't she? She had had to work so hard. How else could she have given what he needed to be successful, to face the world with a proud head? She had given him the best education, the finest clothes and food, a luxurious home. But he had despised her.

"Goodbye, Mother," he had said that cold autumn day, and he had never looked back.

Rena felt pain in her fingers and realized that she was nearly crushing the music box. She dropped it on the soft carpet and scrambled on hands and knees to the cabinet. Trembling, she held the bottle to her lips and closed her eyes, not wanting to see her reflection in the mirror, the image of an old woman so desperate that she could not even wait to pour the drink demurely into a crystal goblet on the sideboard.

The liquor flowed down smoothly, caressingly, and a sweet numbing started, edged inside. It began to calm the raging of her heart, the cutting in her soul. But not enough. Take away that picture, the solitary young man with the willow tree bleeding softly behind him! Oh, God! She stumbled and clutched the hard edge of the dresser.

"Jesus loves me, this I know." The slow tinkling strains wafted up from the floor. "This . . . I . . . know." Silence. She kicked the thing away and took another drink, and another.

Later she awoke, aware of raised voices below. What was she doing on the floor? Rena clutched the sculptured carpet. Honcho and Jack were barking furiously. Then Lenore's voice was shouting at them. Then a little silence. Voices again. A man's voice, unfamiliar yet strangely known.

She pulled herself up and stumbled across the room, closer to the door. She listened. What were they saying? Lenore's painfully refined accents cut the air with the coldness of steel.

"I told you. She does not wish to see you now."

Why not? Lenore hadn't told her anyone was calling. How dare she? Unless. . . . Probably another salesman. Thankfully, she crept toward her bed. Lenore always kept her free from such dreary business. Her head swam, and for a moment she felt herself falling again.

"Miss Kremser, I demand to see my mother immediately!"

Mother? Goodbye, Mother! Rena felt her stomach leap and a chill race through her. Could it be?

Not thinking about the dressing gown partly unbuttoned, her unrestrained silver-red hair falling about her bare shoulders, she flung the door open and grasped the railing of the spiral staircase with one hand. What was in her other hand? Something cold, smooth, hard.

She looked down from her little balcony at the people below. Lenore whirled around, her eyes transformed by open shock. There in a little circle of lamplight he stood, tall, slender, looking up at her through those blue, blue eyes, so like his father's. Something flashed in them. Pity? Disgust? Hate? Had he come to recount her list of sins?

"Mother!" The blue eyes bore through her.

Handsome he was, with a touch of silver at the temples and his light hair and beard sort of golden, luminous. He was youth and beauty and goodness. Once she had held it all in her arms. Now it seemed to mock her, to laugh at her from its unreachable pinnacle.

"Mother?" The voice was incredulous, a little more than a whisper.

"What are you staring at?" she demanded. Her voice sounded strange to her ears. It was as though she were listening to a tape recording played back. She listened, amazed at the voice so unlike her own. "Haven't you ever seen a drunken woman before? Here! *Here!*" She raised the glass bottle in her left hand. "I think there's a drop or two left! Would you be having a drink with me?"

Laughter, high-pitched, sensual. Was it hers?

He was leaning toward her on the steps. She could see the lean, tanned arms reaching, the golden hairs on the back of his hands. And suddenly she could see nothing more.

She felt herself falling on something soft and fragrant, like the pine-needle bed she had loved to stretch out on as a child in the forest near her home. Maybe she was dead and had been granted a little spot of rest from the clamor of the world.

All right. Let it be so. She was too tired to get up anymore.

seven

> The smiles that win, the tints that glow,
> But tell the days in goodness spent,
> A mind at peace with all below,
> A heart whose love is innocent!
>
> LORD BYRON

Richard lay only half awake; something in his troubled subconsciousness was unwilling to surface. It had been a long, restless night after his visit to the stone mansion and he had seen Rena for the first time in fifteen years.

He hadn't dared hope for a warm reunion, but neither had he been prepared for what he found. Could that strange, blue-green visage with red hair flying coarse and wild around a florid face really be his mother? Had she, in her drunken stupor, even recognized her own son?

"Would you be having a little drink with me?" she had asked sensually, her body draped over the upstairs rail, a half-drained bottle raised in her hand.

He had torn his eyes away from her, feeling the agony of childhood loneliness all over again. He could only incredulously whisper "Mother," before he had left her house, the big gray dogs leering and growling as they had lunged against their chains. They too had rejected him and had bore him ill will.

Now, after a long night of restlessness, the day was well in progress. A bright flash of sunlight beamed in the window, warmed his face, and then in seconds was gone as the cloud cover snuffed it out.

Richard showered and put on a pair of new jeans and a plaid shirt. As he ate breakfast on the porch of his cabin, he tried not to think at all about what had occurred or about what he would do. But somehow the plans formed in his mind as some logical part of him took over.

He would meet with her when she was sober and discuss in civil terms the problems of Pinewood Acres. He owed her that much. Then if she told him to go, he would. Undoubtedly it was Rena's fault that the resort was in trouble. Still, he wondered if she might be a victim, not only of her own alcoholism but of greed from some force beyond herself. In her condition she was vulnerable. There were always those who preyed on the weakness of others.

Lenore's angular face with its smooth frame of hair sprang into his mind. Why would a woman of her sophistication stay with a drunken old woman whose business was failing? Something in her too kind, too cultured demeanor unnerved him. Yet, hadn't she in some measure protected Rena from a watching world? Hadn't she been the one to look after Rena when family members had been distant and silent? She had tried to dissuade him from his visit last night, to keep him from seeing his mother in that dreadful condition.

Richard had kicked away the detestable bottles, the clutter of glasses and papers. "Why do you let her go on like this? Why don't you get her some help?" he had screamed at Lenore as he watched her put his mother to bed.

Lenore's eyes had held his in icy silence as he leaned toward his mother who staggered like some crazed creature unable to care for herself. He had been appalled and ashamed but glad that she had forsaken the name Ogden. Instead she carried the name Mara, her second husband's name. Could the name have its origin in the biblical word *marah*, meaning bitter? Had some ironic fate dealt her the title that best fit her?

He swallowed against the unpleasant taste in his mouth. Why had he come here? Why should he care at all? Was it that inexplicable bond between a child and mother that held him? He wanted to pack up his things and head for Minneapolis, to forget that he had seen her, to live his life, as he always had done, apart from her. Perhaps that is precisely what he would do!

But what would become of her? Would she die a wretched old woman for whom no one cared? What friend would mourn her? Lenore? He felt an involuntary shiver.

"How long has she been like this?" he had asked, glaring into Lenore's green eyes as he bent over Rena's unconscious body in the trail of aqua silk.

"She went to the club this afternoon. She'll sleep it off and be quite herself in the morning," Lenore had told him with cold professionalism. "I'll take care of her." Lenore had lifted Rena with amazing effortlessness and placed her on the bed. Amid the clutter of bottles and junk had been a ceramic piece in the form of a mother with a child. The thing had lain on its side with the mother's gentle smile ludicrous against the stained carpet.

Richard had slammed the door to the liquor cabinet. "And why in heaven's name do you let her have this garbage right here in the room?" he had shouted.

Lenore had wheeled around, her smooth black hair following unruffled, like a snake's skin refusing to be shed. "And what would you have me do? I'm an employee here.

I don't make moral judgments about my employer."

"This has nothing to do with moral judgments. She's going to kill herself. Can't you see that?"

Her eyes had held his in unflinching disgust. Then abruptly Lenore had left the room, leaving him there with the sleeping woman and the stench of stale bourbon.

Her eyes had hurled the accusation as surely as if her grim lips had spoken it. Rena was his mother, not hers. Indeed, where had he been while his mother was slowly destroying herself? The unanswered letters could hardly have been his excuse. He should have come long ago. But why had she not answered him or asked her personal secretary to write?

The guilt that tore at him further estranged him from the wholeness he longed to experience within himself and . . . and what? The cosmos? God? He couldn't tell. And the thing bore down on him now with such oppression that he felt incapable of sorting it all out.

He drained his cup of cold coffee and, grabbing his windbreaker, set off toward the high outcropping of rocks that lined the distant coast.

Clouds hanging low over the tops of hills projected a strange inner shining that could not be hidden behind their gray bulges. The breeze winging through the leaves like capricious birds held a hint of rain. Then suddenly the sun burst forth like a great golden eagle, seeming to dry the mist with flaps of its outrageous wings. The hide-and-seek game between the clouds and the sun continued as he ventured farther away from the cabins.

He sauntered down the coast toward the cove of sharp piled rock and bleached sand. Exploding prisms of light from the sky players danced and glowed in the turquoise lake. Then, as though a rest period had been declared, a calm settled across the expanse, and the reflection of trees on the opposite shore shone in the glasslike water.

But quickly the hide-and-seek game took on a rougher aspect, threatening, dark. Maybe he had been foolish to set off so far from his cabin with only a windbreaker for protection. But he walked on in that careless oblivion of one wrestling with greater dangers than wind and rain.

Higher and higher on the rocky coast he climbed, exhilarated by the wind that seemed to carry some inexplicable treasure in its arms. Presently he realized that he was not the only tourist to seek the high cove. A painter with an easel propped up on the rocks sat on a folding denim stool, her back to him, her red blouse blowing out like the crimson sail on a solitary boat. She seemed a part of it all, carried on the arms of the wind, as natural as the rocks and the trees.

He moved nearer, drawn by her light brown hair, ruffled by the gusts of wind, blowing in waves about her shoulders. Brush in hand, she gazed out upon the brooding lake. Perhaps her deep thought kept her unaware of his approach, he thought.

Richard stopped, suddenly arrested by a sense of the familiar. Something in the delicate arc of her arm and fingers as she held the brush startled him. Something in the lift of her head, in the fine light hair. . . .

Suddenly he heard the gentle aria he had heard that morning in the woods. He stood still, watching and remembering the pureness of the face he had seen that day, the shining gold in her eyes, the arms uplifted to embrace a willow branch. He knew, although she had not turned or become aware of his presence, that she was the same young woman he had come upon that early morning as he had climbed to glimpse the stone mansion.

Richard folded his arms over the windbreaker and confronted himself sternly. It had to be the idyllic quality of this place, or some deep yearning of his own heart, that had temporarily taken over his reason.

"Hello!" he called in a friendly, casual way.

She whirled around and in so doing dislodged the little aluminum pail near her easel. "Oh!" Her eyes registered surprise, and Richard was sorry that he hadn't warned her of his presence earlier.

"I'm sorry. Didn't mean to sneak up on you." He rescued the pail that perched precariously near the edge of the top group of rocks.

Her blouse of vibrant red loosely covered her swimming suit, giving strong contrast to the creamy whiteness of her skin. The luminous eyes he remembered from his vantage point in the woods searched his in a testing way. She seemed to be satisfied and smiled as she took the water pail.

"I—just didn't expect anyone so far off the beaten path."

The little trek to retrieve the pail had given him the time needed to recover his usual good sense. He dropped his hands loosely into his pockets and moved a little closer to view the scene on her easel.

"It's good," he pronounced. "Winslow Homer would be proud of you. I'm Richard Ogden, a guest at the resort."

The golden light danced in her eyes as she returned his smile. "Angie Carlson, also a guest. I've probably not seen you before because I—that is, we—haven't been here long."

We? wondered Richard. Of course. Anyone as lovely as

she would belong to someone. Richard studied the sweeping pastels on her painting. Angie. For Angela, no doubt. Angel. She had seemed like an angel that morning in the woods.

"My friend and I came here together. Unfortunately, she learned just the day after our arrival that her father has had a heart attack. She's gone to be with him." Her voice softened with sympathy.

"A terrible thing to happen, especially on your holiday." He was touched by her solitariness. "I hope he's much better now."

Thunder rumbled from some distant corner of sky as the wind tugged at their clothing and threatened to dismantle her easel and painting. Angie began to gather her things.

"I should have headed back long before now," she said.

"I was afraid that a storm was brewing in those clouds. Here, let me get that." Richard helped her zip the portfolio and secure the aluminum easel legs in their straps.

"Thanks." She thrust an assortment of brushes inside a vinyl pouch on the case. "It serves me right getting caught in the rain. Sometimes when I paint, I lose track of time, and weather."

The first torrent unleashed itself with surprising strength. Richard scooped up his windbreaker and placed it over Angie's shoulders. "Here. This will help some. Let me carry that." He bundled the ungainly equipment under his arm and took hold of her hand, wet and cold with rain.

The rocks under their feet were slippery and the noise of the vehement storm was deafening, but they quickly climbed down the rocky slope. Electric flashes spit and cracked, growing nearer and more frequent. It would be better to head for the resort than to seek the shelter of trees.

His jacket hung long and enormous on Angie's small frame. He grinned over his shoulder. "It's not a perfect fit, but maybe it will keep you from getting pneumonia."

"But you'll be soaked through," she protested loudly over the noise of the storm.

"Don't worry!" he said, laughing. "Watch that ledge!"

They hurried down the slope, and soon the gravel path provided flat, even travel. They passed the forest and the golf course and rounded the curve where the rows of cabins stood with shimmering eyes.

"I'm on the first row, second cabin. Come on," she called breathlessly. She pulled ahead of him, dropping his hand.

Funny how warm her hand had seemed in his. Richard followed her into the cabin and set the portfolio and easel down near the door. A puddle of water from his clothing quickly collected on the dark green tile.

"Thanks," she said, grabbing a towel from the rack in the kitchen. "Here, take this." She handed it to him just as another clap of thunder rocked around them and a surprisingly luminous flash of lightning cracked sharply near the cabin door.

"Please! Come in! I'll get a blanket." Her teeth were chattering as she scurried toward an adjoining room and returned with a quilt that she draped over his shoulders as a mother might do for a child who had played too long in a puddle.

"No need to go to this trouble," he began.

"Don't be silly. The least I can do is fix you a hot drink. And you can't go back out in that storm with that lightning going on."

He wrapped the blanket around himself and removed his

soaked boots and set them near the door. He lit a match to the kindling in the fireplace and watched the tiny flame flicker tentatively.

She returned wearing a green wool sweater and jeans. She had combed her wet hair back from her face, but a few drying tendrils curled softly against her moist cheeks. It seemed to Richard that she was like the morning newly risen.

The first few flames rose uncertainly in the fireplace. Richard felt their quick warmth as he urged the adjoining logs closer to one another.

"I'll hang your jacket on the mantel. It'll be dry soon. I hope you haven't caught your death of something."

She seemed suddenly shy, as though only now aware of a strange man in her living room, drying himself by the fire. She gave a little shrug and looked down at her fingers. "I'll just get us some coffee."

Richard sat down on the vinyl chair near the fire and watched her move around in the kitchen, setting cookies on a plastic tray and filling mugs with coffee. Such ordinary actions, yet he sensed something quite extraordinary in her that he could not have identified, something beautiful and innocent.

She brought the refreshments in and set them on a low table by the flower-print couch. She sat at the end closest to his chair with the table between them.

He regarded her over the edge of his cup. She was young with the clear-eyed look of a trusting child, but she had the demeanor of a woman who knew what life was about and how to make her way in it.

He let his eyes play over her hands, not consciously looking for a ring, but marking well that there was none.

For a brief moment his wife's face flashed before his eyes, the way she had looked at him when he knew that she had no longer kept the vows of their marriage. Maybe he had expected too much. Maybe trust was something that really didn't exist, except in the most fanciful of dreams. Maybe love was also only a myth. But that was too sad to contemplate.

He looked up to find her watching him, an expression of concern touching her face. Richard set the cup down, unnerved. Wasn't daydreaming a pastime of old men? But what he felt now as he met her eyes was something akin to a schoolboy's bewildered young emotions, something for which he hadn't had the time or inclination in many years.

"This is a beautiful resort, isn't it? Have you been here before?" Her luminous eyes warmed him.

"No, I—" He began to explain that he was visiting his mother who owned the resort, but into his mind flashed the image of Rena leering drunkenly from the rail. The words died in his throat. "This is . . . my first visit. I . . . I own an advertising agency in Minneapolis. Just here for a few days' vacation." He recovered himself. "Hopefully thunderstorms are not to be the order of every day around here!"

She laughed in a warm, musical way that touched him, and she poured him another cup of coffee. "I hope not, too. Even Winslow Homer couldn't paint in the rain."

They sat listening to the storm, now a slow, disgruntled rumbling and tapping, like a feeble old man not to be taken seriously. The fire blazed in full flame, crackling and brilliant, and between him and Angie stretched a kind of timelessness that Richard could not have explained to himself. She had asked no questions, nor had he, yet he sensed a comfort with her that was fresh and genuine.

"And you? Have you been to Pinewood Acres before?" he asked.

"No. My friend Jen brought me. She knows the owner, Mrs. Mara. They're related. Jen's her niece."

Richard swallowed hard against the coffee and the sudden leaping inside him. Could Jen be Jennifer Flurry, Rena's sister's girl whom he hadn't seen since they were children? She must be the same one he had played with as a boy. He stared at Angie incredulously until he was aware that she was watching him with growing perplexity.

"I see," he responded, collecting himself.

"Yes," she said, still watching him, "Mrs. Mara has been most kind to let us come at what must be only a fraction of the cost. I—I went to thank her."

Richard rose and took a few deliberate pokes at the logs; he needed to look away and take in this strange information. So, she knew Rena, had visited her. Had she seen Rena in the same shameful condition that he had? What would this lovely young woman think if she knew that he was the son of a bitter, drunken woman living in that foreboding stone house?

"They say she drinks too much, that nothing good can come to those who get involved with her and her affairs." Was he really saying this? And more words sounded in his ears. "You ought to stay away from that house, you know. There's something sinister about—"

He stopped himself, seeing the sudden alarm in Angie's eyes. He laughed nervously and shrugged off his words as though they had been a joke. A very poor joke, he thought.

He continued, attempting a casual, offhand manner. "You know how people talk. You're much too lovely to spend your time in haunted houses with old women."

But there was no answering lightness in Angie's words, nor any hint that she was pleased with the compliment. "She's very lonely, I think," she said quietly. "I guess her husband died some time ago, and her only son doesn't give her much attention. It's too bad. People shouldn't neglect their parents when they're old. I felt very sorry for her."

Crackling flames accosted the stillness; the thunder had stopped and the rain was slowly ending. Richard drew in his breath slowly and replaced the poker in its stand.

"I guess the world is filled with lonely people, but not with enough people to care." He did not look at her but carefully folded the blanket that had warmed and dried him. Then he looked at her deliberately, wanting to say that she was special, good, beautiful, but no words came. Most young women would be affected by such words of flattery. But she had thought only of another's need.

"I think the rain has stopped. I'll go now," he said softly without moving. It was as though they both knew their meeting was coming to an end and that perhaps they would never see each other again.

"Thanks for the fire and the coffee." He took his windbreaker from the hanger and went to the door. She followed and smiled in that clear, unaffected way. Did she know how different she was from most women?

"Thanks for . . . for your kindness," she said.

He took the slender hand that she held out to him and held it gently, wondering sadly why life could not offer its sweetest gifts when it was possible or permissible to accept them.

eight

So when the close of pleasure's day
To gloom hath near consign'd us
We turn to catch one fading ray
Of joy that's left behind us.

THOMAS MOORE

Angie huddled in her sweater as she watched the early morning mists rise and hover over the lake. They seemed to be brooding, pondering some difficulty, perhaps remembering when their dark forebears had covered the face of the deep on that day of beginnings. Slowly they thinned, drifted, dissipated. Gradually the sun erased all evidence of their presence.

She shivered, anticipating the first warm rays of the sun on her back. She hadn't gone to the cove today but had chosen to watch the sunrise over the lake from the boat landing. The water had risen high after yesterday's storm, but now it lay calmly, with only the slightest soft lapping against the docks.

She liked that gentle sound; it reminded her of Bess, the cat she had loved as a child. Bess had given birth to several litters and cared for each kitten with native tenderness, licking its newness with steady strokes of her efficient pink tongue. But Bess never lost her primal instincts. When she was stalking a bird or a chipmunk, she could lash out with terrorizing quickness, leap upon her prey, and tear it to shreds with flashing teeth and claws. It was the way of Nature; those sharp contrasts never ceased to astound her.

In just such a way the storm had burst upon them yesterday, but thinking about it now brought a powerful remembrance: the pressure of Richard Ogden's strong arm around her and the warmth of his hand and windbreaker as he guided her down the rocky slopes. She had been surprised at how safe she had felt, how unafraid . . . even inviting him into her cabin. It had been a rash and careless thing to do, for she had never laid eyes on him before. Yet at the time it had seemed natural, neighborly even.

Their talk had been light and easy, with none of the intrusiveness or subtle bantering that often characterized the young men she had met. Something was different about Richard Ogden, something deep and thoughtful that attracted and troubled her all at once. She walked along the lakeside now, watching the action at the water's surface and the way the sun's rays danced in the little ripples, all silvery and shining, like memories of happy moments for which one should be glad and not try to imprison.

After breakfast she headed for the resort office. Surely today there would be some word from Jen, she thought. She had written to her, describing her visit to Aunt Rena, but she had been gentle in the detailing of events. There was no need to give Jen any further cause for concern, and there was little that either of them could do for her anyway, wasn't there?

Rena Mara was so like those helpless ones like Eddie, Roslyn, and old Jack, the part-time janitor who could never remain sober for longer than a few weeks. She pictured him now as she had seen him so often in her four years at the mission, with his old Dodger's cap, as faded as his hair, shading brown eyes that were always dreaming of what might have been and what almost was.

Angie had covered for him frequently when he hadn't shown up, doing the janitor work even when she was exhausted from her own job. But the Packetts had no other choice; eventually they had to fire old Jack. Angie walked slowly toward the resort's office, wishing that she could erase those dark, dreamy eyes from her heart, those indelible marks of one more failure.

She entered the office lobby and approached the desk. "Anything for Angie Carlson today?" she asked the young woman who was leafing through a stack of receipts behind the counter.

"Be with you in just a moment." The willowy clerk had frizzy hair and a broad nose with a wide field of freckles sprinkled across it. She did not look up when Angie entered but continued to thumb through the sheaf of papers spread in front of her. The telephone rang twice, then three times. With exasperation the woman stopped in her search and swept up the receiver. She gave a helpless shrug of her shoulders.

Angie smiled her sympathy and stepped away to look at the pamphlets in the wooden rack. The attractive brochures advertised sightseeing excursions and local attractions. Angie scanned these as she waited, thinking how little she would enjoy going on one of these trips alone.

A door opened across from her, and Angie glanced up to see an ebony-haired woman emerge from the manager's office, the office of Harrington Riggs, who had entertained her with coffee only the day before. Lenore Kremser paused and fixed surprised green eyes on Angie.

"Oh—Miss Carlson," she said with a sudden graceful turn. The skirt of Lenore's dress with its deeply tailored pleats flared, revealing slender legs and delicate ankles. Lenore touched a hand to her usually flawless hair, now uncharacteristically mussed. She blushed as she smoothed a stubborn pleat that had become dislodged.

Undoubtedly the two, Lenore and Harrington Riggs, often had business to discuss. Angie looked back at the door but Lenore had closed it adroitly behind her.

"I trust you are well and enjoying your stay here?"

Angie found this high-sounding professionalism strange and disquieting. They were, after all, women of the same generation. "Hello, Lenore," she said wearily. "Please, won't you call me Angie?"

"Of course, Angie."

"I'm enjoying it here very much. But, tell me, how is Mrs. Mara? Is she feeling better?"

"Mrs. Mara is resting comfortably today. I'm sure she'd be pleased that you asked," Lenore responded without warmth.

The office door suddenly opened, and Harry Riggs stepped out looking like a neatly trimmed torpedo, his white shirt open at the neck to reveal a dark growth of curly hair and a gleaming gold chain. He approached them grinning, a look of pleasure in his eyes.

"Well, Angie, good morning. How was the shopping yesterday?" He clapped a hand on her shoulder and gave her a deliberate smile, but even as she began to respond, Riggs turned his smile on Lenore, who was staring at him with vague contempt.

"Angie is a rather special guest, Lenore," Riggs said, "I understand that she's even paid a sick call on our eminent landlady."

Angie stepped back a little, disturbed by the tension between the two and by the cynical tone in Riggs's voice.

Riggs turned those steely blue eyes back to Angie with a look of apology. "You will be sure to let us know if there is anything we can do to assist you here at Pinewood Acres. I'm sure Lenore will do all that she can to see that you have a pleasant stay, won't you, Lenore?"

The two had been engaging in some kind of dispute, Angie felt sure. A lover's quarrel? The tousled hair and the look of wounded dignity in Lenore's expression seemed to indicate that. Anyway, it irritated her to be the foil, and she was eager to get away. The woman behind the desk was motioning to her, waving an envelope in her hand. "If you'll excuse me," Angie said as she left them to get her letter.

But Harrington Riggs's expression froze suddenly as another guest entered the lobby. The laconic smile disappeared from Harry's tan face. Abruptly he dropped his eyes to his shoes, strode into his office, and closed the door. Angie watched Lenore also disappear behind the desk area, her head thrown back and her heels making deliberate attacks on the tile floor.

Angie turned to see Richard Ogden framed in the glass doorway. A sudden catch in her throat caught her off guard. She had hoped to see him again, but now she felt shy, uneasy, and confused by Harry's behavior.

Richard was smiling in her direction, his eyes shining with startling blueness. "Hello," he said warmly, stopping a short distance away and resting an elbow on the desk. He appeared not to notice the abrupt departure of Lenore and the adroit closing of Harrington Riggs's door.

He was wearing gray slacks and a shirt the color of a summer afternoon's sea. His hair and beard were like wheat on a still day when the sun shines with singular warmth and color. "How are you?" he was asking. "No ill effects from the storm, I hope."

She smiled. "No. How about you? I'm the one who had the jacket." They were both silent a moment.

"Good news?" he asked, nodding to the letter in her hand.

"Oh, I don't know. Just now got it." She tore the envelope open and silently read the note.

Dear Angie,

Father is to be moved out of ICU today. It was touch and go for a while, but the doctors think that he's going to be fine after some rest and recuperation. Mom's okay, now that Dad's better. I'll drop you a line in a day or two when we see how he gets along. I hope I can return to Pinewood soon.

Love,
Jen

Angie folded the letter and replaced it in the envelope, grateful for Jen's good news and for the hope that she might be back soon. "It is good news," she said, looking up. "Jen's father is getting well. Thank God," she finished softly.

Angie stood facing Richard, who regarded her with those intensely blue eyes now warmed by some inner light. She put the letter in her purse, sensing a strange feeling of well being that comes at times, a feeling that life is good and genuine.

"Angie," Richard paused, as though assessing his thoughts or trying to frame the right words, "there's a hot-air balloon festival in Haynes this week. Would you like to go over this afternoon? We could take in the race." He shifted his weight and, like a boy who isn't sure what to do, dropped his hands into his pockets.

"A balloon festival! It sounds really exciting." She warmed to his quick look of pleasure.

"Good. Is one o'clock all right?"

She nodded, smiling. "I'll be ready." Angie thanked the desk clerk who had been listening with interest and who now pretended to be very busy with her ledgers. Angie felt a faint reddish blush on her high cheekbones.

As Angie moved away she heard Richard's knock on Harry's door, then at length heard a decidedly stiff response. She wondered vaguely what business Richard might have with Harry and why, if the two knew each other, there had been such obvious avoidance a few moments earlier. Certainly Harrington Riggs's smooth charm was something reserved for selected guests, not Richard.

She followed the path to her cabin, feeling lighthearted and at the same time a little incredulous. Why had she agreed to go with Richard? She wasn't in the habit of making dates with men she hardly knew. Who was this Richard Ogden anyway? She paused on the winding path. If she had any sense she'd turn around and tell him that she'd changed her mind, that she'd not be able to go after all.

Not that there hadn't been other men in her life, even after Rob. But she had had little time to think about relationships with men, for her life had been one of devotion and service to God. It was glad service, at least in the beginning. She had been single-minded in her purpose, seldom missing the things that most young women desire.

"Are you sure this is what you want, dear?" her mother had asked that spring morning so long ago. The question had come when she revealed her plan to devote her life to ministry.

It wasn't easy to describe, even to herself, her sense of calling, her sureness that she was acting in obedience to the will of God. Mother had wanted her to be sure, very sure. Perhaps she had known how rigorous such a life could be, what sacrifices would be required, things Angie could not have guessed.

With gladness she had prepared, studied, and prayed, and there had been joy in that service. She loved leading the children's meetings, planning youth events, teaching about God, and helping people to see how faith could be a vital reality. As Angie walked across the green, tree-lined resort now, she wondered what had happened to that early joy. But she was afraid that she knew after all. She had been unable to show them how faith could work in their lives. They continued in their defeated lives, not seeing, not understanding, often not caring.

Like Rena Mara they continued to miss life, the real life that she was somehow unable to articulate. What would Richard Ogden, a successful advertising executive, think if he knew that he had just made a date with a minister, a minister who wasn't sure any longer who she was and what she would do when this vacation ended?

"Will you come and see me again?" Rena had asked her in a forlorn childish way. She wished that she hadn't visited her in the first place, hadn't witnessed Rena's helplessness, her sadness. That was the sort of thing she had left behind to come here. Here she longed for beauty, order, and peace. She had been through the storm; now she longed for the calm that followed. Perhaps for today she could forget the raging and the defeat and simply enjoy an afternoon with someone who enjoyed her company.

nine

. . . There's mercy in every place,
And mercy, encouraging thought!
Gives even affliction a grace
And reconciles man to his lot.

William Cowper

Summer hung on like a performer, fingers tight on the trapeze of the world. She flew, a golden arc through the azure sky, her hair draping the treetops, gilding everything she touched. The world, like an adoring crowd, held its breath, fearing to applaud lest her concentration be broken, lest she fall away and crumple in a dying heap at its feet. It would await the artist's final flourish, the perfect descent of her dainty feet, the low sweeping bow and the upward appeal of face and fingers. The light of her presence would sustain through a hundred frozen days.

It was that kind of day as Angie sat next to Richard, watching the exquisite performance through the open car window. She exulted in the wonder and beauty around them. They had traveled for several minutes in companionable silence when Richard had turned to her, a cautious smile above his carefully groomed beard.

"I'm so glad that Jennifer's father is better." He swept his glance back to the road in time to swerve around a car that had pulled suddenly onto the highway in the moment his eyes had been averted.

Jennifer? Had she mentioned Jen's real name? Angie wondered. She couldn't recall speaking of her friend as anything but Jen. Curious. He'd probably simply assumed that Jen stood for Jennifer, not Jeanette or Genevieve. She smoothed the folds of her yellow flowered skirt.

"Me too," she said wistfully. "We had such plans for this vacation, things we wanted to do together. I really miss her. But her letter indicated that she might be able to return very soon!"

"That's . . . wonderful," Richard remarked without gusto, his eyes intent on the highway.

Angie was puzzled over the sudden frown that disappeared as quickly as it had come.

"Have you been friends long?" he was asking.

"Ever since college. We work in the same city and enjoy doing things together." She paused, thinking about Jen, her charm, her vibrant enjoyment of life. "Friends just don't come any finer than Jen."

Richard didn't respond and the expression in his forward-looking gaze was inscrutable, but Angie still felt at ease. They shared light, happy conversation, warm in each other's tacit promise not to pry. Angie related the story of the ski trip she and Jen had taken to Colorado the preceding year and how Jen had sprained her ankle her first time down the beginner slope.

"We still laugh about it," Angie explained, "but at the time Jen was furious, not so much because she had to lie around the fire drinking hot chocolate and receiving the sympathy of everyone in the lodge, but because she had spent so much money for a new ski outfit that would never be worn again, at least not that season."

The balloon fair proved to be a gala event of vibrant color. Great bulging bubbles with bold stripes and scallops rose high above the trees, riding the wind higher and higher until they seemed to be childish toys in the ocean of sky. Booths displayed miniature hot-air balloons, key rings, notepads, books describing the history of ballooning, posters, and trinkets of every description.

A series of drawings and scripts outlined the fascinating story of Jacques-Etiénne and Joseph-Michel Montgolfier, two French brothers who had been impressed by the way in which scraps of paper soared up the chimney over an open household fire. They decided to place toy balloons made of paper bags over small dishes filled with burning charcoal. Noting how these bags rose to the ceiling then dropped slowly to the floor as the air inside them cooled, the brothers decided to make large balloons and fill them with hot air.

From that curious beginning, the Montgolfier brothers' first balloon filled with warm air ascended from Versailles, France, in 1783. At first the Montgolfiers sent sheep and chickens and other barnyard creatures aloft in their balloons. Then Pilatre de Rozier and the Marquis d'Arlandes went up in a Montgolfier creation fastened to the ground by a long rope. The two brothers and other interested experimenters made many successful exhibition flights as they continued to develop the lighter-than-air craft.

Angie thought that it might have been on a day such as this that the first balloon ascended, and she thrilled to the intriguing story as they read about it. Hand in hand, they moved among the throngs of sightseers, at one with that sense of experience that leaves one breathlessly glad for life and a little in awe of it.

Holding hands came quite naturally, and it was the only practical way to avoid being separated in the pressing crowds. She was sure that Richard didn't give it a thought, but she was surprised at how glad she was for the warmth and closeness of him.

They lunched in a little sidewalk cafe where umbrellas formed an old-world shelter over them. They ordered hamburgers and tall glasses of iced tea that came crystal-cubed, dripping, and carrying a circle of lemon on the amber lip of each glass.

Later they watched the balloons rise in the blue reaches of space, feeling the warmth of the sun on their heads and shoulders. Angie couldn't remember a time when she had felt more at ease in the world and singularly touched by a simple, noble beauty. She looked across the table at Richard, who was looking past her, a quizzical expression on his face, as though some idea had struck him.

"Angie, would you like to go up? In a balloon, I mean?"

Something of boyish wonder made his eyes leap. Angie had seen the sign advertising a balloon ride over the city. She started to say something about how expensive it would be, but checked herself. Richard Ogden most likely didn't need to worry about money, and if he did, he undoubtedly would not like to be reminded.

"You're not afraid of heights, are you?" he asked, leaning excitedly across the table.

"No, but I've never ridden in one before. I guess I never thought I might actually have the chance to." Angie could feel the pulse of her excitement matching the gleam in his eye. "Let's do it!" She rose simultaneously with Richard and they grasped hands in eager delight.

The world fell away beneath them, and they were suddenly propelled into a different existence, a place where time and memories and things ceased to be. There was now and never and forever and always and the blue infinity engulfing and swallowing everything and everyone. Angie felt Richard's arm close around her shoulders, felt the insane longing to remain in that timeless moment, uncluttered, unquestioned, free. Suddenly she felt overwhelmed, and she heard the strange tight sound of her own voice in a choked little cry.

Richard's arm tightened and drew her near enough so that she could feel the cold hardness of his chest.

"I'm not afraid, really," she said breathlessly. "It's just so . . . grand, so lofty!"

"I know. It makes you feel like Adam must have felt when he first opened his eyes and saw the sky."

"All clean and clear and unspoiled," Angie whispered, suddenly struck with a sense of awe and at the same time with her own minuteness.

"Wouldn't it be great if the world could be this way, clean and unspoiled, I mean?" Richard paused, his eyes luminous. Then abruptly his voice dropped. "Only in dreams, I'm afraid. The real world is something else."

"I know." Angie knew only too well the evidences of a stained universe. Little Eddie with his trusting heart had been victim. Oh, the dirt, the disease, the terror, the raging. How Eddie would love to be here! She closed her eyes, recalling the dreadful dream of the evil butterfly, the deep abyss, and her heart reached up in faith as Roslyn's face clouded her vision. Oh, yes, some day things would be different.

"It will be this way again, clean and whole, I mean,"

she whispered then. "But not until He comes back."

They drifted in blue stillness. "You mean at the end of the world, I suppose," he said softly.

"Yes, when Christ returns and a new kingdom of righteousness begins."

He looked at her strangely. "You really believe that?"

"It will be so one day, Richard. I know it. It's what He promised." Angie's words spilled out in a vibrant rush of faith. "God made a perfect world. But sin came in with its dreadful consequences. He redeemed it at such an incredible price, and one day He'll return to rule. It will be perfect again, perfect like all this seems!" Angie felt that she could close her eyes and imagine at that moment the new and beautiful universe, the kingdom of love and light, where the naive and vulnerable need not fear.

They rode on in thoughtful silence, but soon the earth drew nearer; they were coming to the end of the ride. Closer and closer the world came with its throngs of people, its buildings, clutter, litter, and dirt. And Richard, still with his arm lightly around her, was thoughtful, distant.

Angie sighed. Now that he probably thought that she was some kind of fanatic, he was likely to avoid her. The degree of her sadness at that prospect surprised her. Well, perhaps it was for the best. Still, she felt tears rising, whether from the emotional experience of the awesome expanse or from some innate sense of lost moments that would never come again, she didn't know.

"What a great ride. I'm glad you went with me," Richard said as they walked away from the open field. "Thanks for making it so special." Once again she couldn't read that expression. Was it a farewell speech or was that wondering, searching look meant to convey appreciation or interest?

The day danced itself into a sort of dazed languor. Golden, sleepy, and satisfied it rested on the hills and dreamed its singular dream. Angie lay her head back on the vinyl seat and wondered at her own sense of simple happiness. She knew that Richard was watching her from the corners of those blue eyes, and she could sense the gentleness of his lips curved in an enigmatic smile.

They had eaten sandwiches and tea in a small coffee shop and now pulled into Pinewood Acres. Long slants of dying light turned the lake golden and meditative. They parked in the guest lot and walked silently toward the long rows of cabins.

"It's been a lovely day, Richard," she said as they approached her cabin. "Thank you. I'll never forget the ride. It was magnificent."

"Will I see you tomorrow?" he asked quietly, his hands in his pockets, his eyes touching hers briefly and dropping away.

She gave a little shrug, aware of her quickening pulse. She was surprised at herself, realizing that she wanted to see him always, wanted all other yesterdays and tomorrows to be swallowed up. Her heart was pounding now with all this unexpected feeling, with the knowledge of its own vulnerability. "I . . . I don't know."

"You're not leaving yet, are you?" he asked. And a startled look sprang into his eyes.

"No." She fixed her eyes on the blue and pink line that separated the lake from the sky. They were like two planets, their rotation suspended, poised by some gravitational force. Each would be drawn to a separate point of origin, and soon the memory of their brief encounter would wane.

She turned away sadly, not wanting to witness the separation or to see the look of farewell on his face. Her voice was husky as she spoke. "Thanks for a wonderful day. Good night, Richard." And she slipped inside the cabin, leaving him standing under the silver crest of the rising moon.

She hadn't invited him in or even given him a friendly kiss on the cheek to indicate her appreciation for the wonderful time he had provided. That would have been the expected thing to do perhaps, the thing she had done many times before. But this time . . . Angie couldn't articulate what was different. It was all too deep, too special.

But she knew that she was vulnerable, lonely. Dear God, she had been so alone and bearing such heavy burdens for so long. There must be time for friendship and for mutual understanding, not this breathless attraction that could be so dangerous.

She lay for a long time thinking of the vast stretches of sky with the luminous clouds, the air so clear that it seemed to transfuse and resurrect the soul. Faith was like that. She remembered how the great wind of the Spirit had blown through her, His purifying breath filling her with Himself. She had felt what it is like to be clean and clear and unspoiled, just as she had felt contemplating the heavens in the balloon.

Her service had grown out of her love for Him. And she would gladly continue if only she could see some evidence that her service was accepted? What caused her to feel such turmoil inside? She didn't want to go back, she knew that. She wanted to stay here forever. The pain and the suffering were more than she could bear. The Eddies of the world were too much for her.

She should have known that she couldn't do it. Had she mistakenly thought in her girlish, sentimental way that God had something for her to do? Had she confused her own ambition for God's voice? And why did Eddie have to die? Why didn't God speak to her now and plainly tell her? But He was silent, . . . or His voice was muffled in the multitude of songs and sorrows that lingered in the tall grasses and the shadowy trees. The cicadas hummed on in the thickness of the night, part of the mystery and madness of life.

ten

. . . Our meddling intellect
mis-shapes the beauteous forms of things. . .
William Wordsworth

The night was windless and heavy, as though the heat of the day had been caught and trapped somehow. A strange night for northern Wisconsin, where the cool breezes usually brought comfort. The birds were silent; even the lake loons held their peace. Richard glanced at his watch; it was past midnight now. This was the only way. He dug through his duffel bag for a flashlight and grabbed his tweed jacket. With its dark, mottled coloring the jacket would make him less visible. He had worn it to the balloon fair. Angie had told him that she liked it, and when she had run her fingers over the fabric of his sleeve he had felt strangely warm.

He switched off the lamp in his cabin and walked out; in a moment the door closed behind him with a little dull tap of the screen against the wood frame. It was a desolate sound, and Richard felt ill at ease as he moved into the darkness.

The pudgy night clerk whom everyone called Tinker would be snoring by now, his stubby feet propped up on the desk. It was a risk, but Richard had to get into that office and look around. It was clear that no one was going to let him look at the books, and he had no right to demand it. He had tried the friendly route with Harry, but that had failed miserably. Right or wrong, he had to get into that office. He found himself at the rear of the building where the yellow lights from the front office cast dim shadows.

Why couldn't Rena accept the truth that he wanted to help her, that in his heart he longed to make life better for her, to make up for the past maybe? He wasn't even sure himself why he felt it so important to help, but she was his mother and she needed him, whether she knew it or not. His suspicion that all was not well here had grown swiftly and ominously in the short time since coming to Pinewood. Something was very wrong, and whether Rena wanted to or not, he had to find out what was causing the business failure and who was at fault.

Harrington Riggs, coldly polite, had made it clear that Richard was not welcome at Pinewood Acres. Riggs had refused to discuss the financial difficulties of the resort and had reminded Richard that it was none of his business.

"Look, man, she's my mother!" Richard had told him desperately.

"Yeah? Well, the way she tells it, you're no son to her! She doesn't want anything to do with you." He had grinned rather menacingly and had seemed to enjoy himself as he went on. "The lady doesn't trust you, Ogden. So, why don't you just butt out!"

Lenore was no help either. Had she even given his letters to Rena? There was no way to know about the letters if Rena wouldn't talk, and she was definitely hostile toward him. It hadn't been only the liquor talking that night he had gone to see her. Drinking had only released her tongue and all the bitterness of her soul.

Riggs was right; she didn't trust him. Well, perhaps she was justified in her attitude. Still, if he could only make her understand, if he could just talk with her when she wasn't stoned out of her mind!

Richard had surveyed the resort the other day when he had visited Riggs. He had tried to memorize every detail so that he could find his way in the dark. He traced his fingers along the lining of his jacket for the slender steel file he had bought. The desk drawers were certain to be locked.

The resort area was deserted, vacationers and staff alike had long since gone to their rest. Richard approached the office, glad for the cover of trees and inadequately trimmed bushes. Surprisingly, the rear door was open, but it led only to a short hallway that contained a janitor's closet and a back door to Riggs's office, which was securely locked.

It seemed an interminable time before the lock yielded to his probing with the instrument, but finally Richard was inside. Tinker's snoring with its rhythmic little snorts and sighs came from the other side of the main door. He'd have to work quickly and hope that Tinker was as dull in sleep as he was in wakefulness.

His fingers had grown numb from the long twisting and probing with the file, and he was sweating inside the tweed jacket. But there was much to do even after gaining entry to the office, and he had no idea what he was looking for. He pulled off his jacket and dropped it in a silent heap on the floor.

With the flashlight held low and its beams shielded by papers to diminish the rays, he searched through cluttered drawers and cabinets. Apparently Riggs wasn't much for organization, judging from the haphazard array of books, letters, and journals. Nearly an hour passed before Richard came upon something that seemed strange to him. Regular payments had been made to a landscaping and lawn care company, exorbitant payments. He took a mental note of the unfamiliar name. His own company employed such a service, but he had never made such high payments for similar work. And from the looks of Rena's resort, little had been done other than what Tinker managed with his lawn mower and hedge clippers.

Richard noticed other inordinately high expenses for services rendered. He grabbed a pencil from the middle drawer and wrote down the names he found. These he could check out later. Could Rena be the victim of one of the oldest tricks in the book, bogus companies with Riggs himself as the payee under a variety of pseudonyms? Surely in her younger days such a scam could never have escaped Rena's careful notice. Even so, it was difficult to imagine that Riggs or anyone else could pull this off.

Richard frowned when the snoring on the other side of the door stopped. Maybe it was just a brief holding of breath from some ecstatic dream. He waited for the crude sounds to resume but instead heard footsteps and a sudden scraping near the door. Richard felt his heart sink.

He quickly replaced the sheaf of papers, tucked his notes in his shirt pocket, and slipped out the rear door. Cicadas rasped in the deep night and the moon cast eerie shadows from narrow pines, but nothing moved and no human sounds could be discerned. Richard straightened and forced himself to walk casually around the office to the front. No need to run now. All was well.

Suddenly out of the darkness the great snarling dogs

leaped, their fangs like silver spikes in the moon glow. Richard fell backward, conscious of a searing pain in his arm which he quickly realized was not caused by canine teeth but by an edge stone at the corner of the building.

"Hey!" he yelled.

A pair of brawny arms pulled the dogs back on long clanking chains. They snarled and growled, their teeth almost fluorescent in the eerie night light.

In an instant Richard was on his feet, looking into the surprisingly calm face of Harrington Riggs. Mock concern spread over the business manager's ruddy features.

"Terribly sorry, old man. The dogs must have taken you for a prowler."

Richard brushed off his pants and folded his arms over his chest, realizing at that instant that he had left his jacket just outside Riggs's office. He steeled himself against a rising panic and maintained a level gaze at the smug-faced Riggs.

"Can't a guest take an evening walk without being accosted around here?" Richard asked, bringing to his voice all the authority and dignity he could manage.

The dogs cringed nearer to their keeper's legs and breathed nervously through clamped jaws.

Riggs gave a grand shrug. "We're not accustomed to guests strolling around past midnight," he said with controlled politeness, "particularly around the office."

"The beasts are a bit far from home, aren't they?" Richard asked coolly.

"Lenore and I got back late from a business meeting. She asked me to walk the brutes. Besides, they do keep prowlers at a distance." Here he paused meaningfully, then added, "Usually."

Richard was repelled by the steely glint of Riggs's eyes and by the ungraciousness of the smile that spread too whitely, too broadly, across the man's face.

"If you've no objection, I'll finish my walk now," Richard said evenly and strode past Riggs and the two restless dogs.

In reply Riggs bent his head slightly in a mock bow and wheeled the dogs around in the direction of the estate house. Even Rena's dogs were under the command of Riggs and Lenore. Strange to have such ferocious beasts around where children and adult guests were vulnerable, Richard thought. He felt the pounding in his chest begin to subside, but the confusion in his mind continued.

There was the question of what to do about his forgotten jacket. Had he left anything in the pockets? Was there any identifying mark? He'd have to go back and retrieve his jacket. But they were sure to be watching the place now. Going back would be impossible. Besides, he was reasonably certain that Riggs knew what he had been doing.

But Riggs was not likely to involve the police in the matter, particularly since no property had been destroyed and nothing had been taken, except some information that might prove dishonesty on his own part. No, Riggs was likely to leave things alone, at least on any official basis.

Still, Richard felt the cold sweat on his face and was aware of a cold that no jacket would have been able to affect. How dangerous was Harrington Riggs? Suppose that the dogs hadn't been restrained? Clearly Riggs meant to scare him off. But if he didn't scare, what then? Richard felt inside his shirt pocket for the little note of scribbled names and wondered what secrets might be contained there.

How hard would it be for a smooth-talking, shrewd businessman to pull the wool over the eyes of a woman whose faculties were clouded by alcohol? Couldn't he take her for everything she had with no one the wiser? Was that what Riggs was up to? And if he had the assistance of a trusted aide who kept the owner mollified and convinced that she was too ill to bother over business matters? If this aide could keep nosy relatives and concerned friends at bay, there was no limit to the money a dishonest person could rake in. And no one would suspect anything except that poor Rena Mara, hopeless alcoholic, had drunk away her savings.

He brooded over this as he made his way back to the cabin. Angie had visited with his mother more than once. The thought of her in that foreboding house with Lenore filled him with a nameless dread. He had only suspected Lenore and Riggs, but they had grown beyond the point of suspicion tonight.

He had warned Angie about going there on that afternoon when the sudden storm had swelled over the land and he had found her on the outcropping of rock above the beach. They had scrambled for shelter like two children caught in an adventure on a summer afternoon. He remembered now how warm her hand had felt in his and how she had smiled when he had wrapped his jacket around her shoulders.

While they had been sipping hot coffee and warming themselves by the fire he had learned that she had come to Pinewood Acres with his cousin Jennifer Flurry and that they were guests of his mother's.

He had wanted to tell her who he was. Something in Angie drew from him a desire for truth. But he hadn't told her. It was utterly shameful to admit, and yet, did his silence put her in jeopardy?

"You ought to stay away from that house. They say that the woman drinks too much, that nothing good can come to those who get involved in her affairs." He had said that then and now he remembered the puzzled eyes of the girl looking back at him.

"She's very lonely," Angie had said simply, ignoring the warning. "People shouldn't neglect their parents when they're old."

And he had felt the shame like a knife in his heart. He was the neglectful son who had allowed his own mother to drink herself into some kind of helpless oblivion. What would Angie have thought of him if she knew that?

Richard walked on as the wind penetrated his thin shirt. Angie was the kind of woman who trusted people, who would help them no matter what the danger to herself. Suppose Riggs assumed that she and he were both out to destroy his plan to make a profit dishonestly? Might Angie also be in danger if she persisted in seeing Rena?

He must convince her to stay away, but how could he do that? What possible reason could he give beyond the weak suggestion given before, without telling her who he was and risking her disapproval?

He had asked to see her again. She had stood there in that saffron dress with the fabric gently swirling in the breeze and her hair highlighted by the rising moon. Her negative response had come with such sharpness and such pain that it had startled him. She hadn't said no exactly. But something in her eyes . . . the sad reticence had been clear.

But why? Why, after such a beautiful day when she had

seemed so happy to be with him? They had walked together all through that afternoon, hand in hand, and with every step and every word he cared more deeply for her.

She was a special person, he knew. She was a Christian, he also knew. He was familiar with the doctrines of the Fall, the Redemption, and the Second Coming. Her allusions to the doctrines had made sense in the balloon as they had looked out over the vast spread of sky.

"Some day it will be perfect again, perfect like all this seems . . . when He returns." She had spoken of the sacrifice to redeem the world, but that was a thing he could not understand. How the light of faith had shone in her beautiful eyes, and how he had longed at that moment to share it with her!

But as yet, faith—at least faith like that—was something to be analyzed, held at bay. He had studied the Christian religion since the yearning to know had come to him after his divorce, since he had known the emptiness of life and all that he had accomplished. But study and analysis had left him empty and weary. The pain of his failure and the knowledge of his sin even now plagued his mind like a great crushing weight.

He wanted to ask her about these things, to look again into those luminous eyes in which something pure and good could not be hidden. Would she see him? She had not seemed interested in seeing him again. It was as though she were telling him goodbye, and yet. . . .

Richard let himself in and lay down on the bed, too weary to undress, his mind whirling with its wonderings and yearnings. If he had known how to pray, he would have done so. As it was, he only lay there bewildered and troubled until sleep overtook him.

eleven

The expense of spirit in a waste of shame
Is lust in action; . . .

WILLIAM SHAKESPEARE

Harry Riggs unleashed Honcho and Jack and hissed at them to get inside the wire fence behind the stone mansion. The dogs protested meekly, then contented themselves at their dish, lapping the water with long, noisy tongues. Harry hooked the latch and peered in at them without seeing them. His thoughts were on other things, and he felt peevish and nervous.

Ogden had been inside his office. Riggs had found the tweed jacket and recognized it at once. The meddling snoop, pretending to be interested in his dear mother's affairs! Had he found anything? What did he intend to do? Riggs turned abruptly and headed toward the house.

Lenore would still be up, even though it was after midnight; he had left her only a short while ago. They had better have a talk about this new development. He cursed Richard Ogden under his breath as he rapped lightly on the back door. That meddling little missionary was a pain in the neck, too. Just when things were where he wanted them!

Lenore appeared at the door wrapped in a white terrycloth robe, her long hair swirling black over her shoulders and her shapely feet encased in black silk slippers with feathery pompoms. Her face was nearly as pale as her robe, for she had removed her make-up in preparation for the night. But the startling effect of white on black struck Harry with a strange force.

"Harry, it's late. You can't come in now!" she said, drawing the cord of her robe around her slim waist.

He shoved her aside and stepped into the kitchen. "Don't give me the schoolgirl shy act! We've got to talk!"

"I mean," she said, drawing herself up angrily, "that she's been restless tonight." Lenore rolled her dark eyes up, to indicate the bedroom where Rena Mara slept. "We don't need her coming down and seeing you here after midnight." Lenore turned her back on him and picked up a glass of juice from the counter. She frowned as she sipped, eyeing Harry over the rim of the glass.

"Well, maybe you'd better keep her door locked from now on." Harry dropped down on a kitchen chair and squinted through narrowed eyes. "Guess who I just found snooping around the office?"

Lenore fixed her eyes on Harry and waited.

"Ogden. Yes, the old lady's kid, come to protect his dear mother!" Riggs grabbed the glass from Lenore and took a long swallow.

"Well, what was he doing?" Lenore asked blandly.

"How should I know!" he snapped. "But you can bet he wasn't just out for a stroll. He came to see me earlier today, demanding to know about the financial state of things around here and to offer his assistance in our crisis!"

Lenore pursed her full mouth, now red from the wine-colored juice she had drunk. "He was pretty demanding when he came to see Rena, too, but I guess he got an eyeful. She practically fell on top of him, and she was so drunk that she couldn't see straight!" Lenore draped her long form over the back of the chair opposite Riggs and looked boldly into his face. "I got her believing he's only after her money. The old lady trusts me. I keep her liquor cabinet well stocked and tell her what a grand old dame she is."

Riggs gave a little smile and thought that Lenore could be deliciously devious. He tugged at a lock of her hair and pulled her face close to his. "You're a good girl."

She was devious, but he knew one thing: she'd do anything for him, the insipid fool. He hated that in her, all the while he used it for his benefit. Now he felt irritated again. "See that nothing happens to change her mind. Keep him away from her, and that nosy little missionary too."

Lenore stood up and turned away from him, swinging her hips with voluptuous indignance. "I rather thought 'she' was your department," his companion said coolly, drawing a bottle from the refrigerator and dropping it down on the counter a little too loudly.

"We've no time for your little jealousies, my pet," Harry said, and, getting up to join her at the counter, he dropped his large hand on top of hers, trapping it there. Her hand throbbed under his, and he liked the way her whole body seemed to respond to his touch. "The fact is that we can pull off this scam as long as we keep busybodies away." He moved his hand, frowning at the floor, as though he'd just come to a decision. "We've about drained all we can off this place."

"Then why can't we just get out of here?" Lenore asked, her voice taking on a plaintive, pleading tone. "I don't like it here, and," Lenore paused and put her arm around Harry's neck, "I'm scared."

Riggs spoke more gently now, although in his gut he felt a churning frustration. "Look, there's nothing to get all uptight about," he began, more to himself than to her. "We've just got to keep our cool. I've got a plan for Miss what's-her-name." He stopped, thinking about the girl with her clear eyes, her winsome softness. It was a shame that such a girl should waste her time visiting sick women and buddying up to a bore like Ogden.

He knew about their trip to the balloon fair. He had seen Ogden's look when he had seen her across the lobby and the way she had stammered and turned pink when he had spoken to her. The two had a thing for each other. Too bad it couldn't keep their minds off Rena and her troubles, but they both seemed preoccupied with the old woman. What had Ogden told her about the resort? Had he shared all his grim suspicions about his poor old mother and her keepers?

He knew about his guests; he made it his business to know. He called Angie Carlson a missionary because he knew she had just come from a little mission church where she was some kind of minister. She was one of those do-gooders who thought that she was placed in this world to save sinners. Those kind of people could cause a heap of trouble. Was Angie Carlson more likely to believe Rena or Ogden? he wondered.

"What sort of plan?" Lenore's question broke in on his jumbled thoughts. "I've done my best to keep her away. It would have been fine, but Rena heard her in the hall and came out. Told the girl to come up. She didn't have any good words about Ogden, though. I was listening at the door and heard it all, even the silly music box she got as a gift."

"Good. Now, what we need to do is reinforce Rena's belief that her son hates her and only wants to look over her money situation and to get a piece of the action. I think—I think I can stimulate that. Let's see."

Lenore sipped her drink thoughtfully, watching him with wary eyes. Her red fingertips clinked irritatingly on the glass.

"Get some of Rena's writing paper, you know, the one with the monogram."

"Now? Why?" she asked incredulously.

"Just do it, and go quietly."

When she returned, Harry dictated the letter he had been framing in his mind over the last few minutes. Several times Lenore looked up with startled eyes, but he urged her back to the paper, reminding her not to write so steadily, but more as a tottering woman with an alcohol problem. When it was done he reviewed it cautiously, then handed it back to Lenore.

"Now read it out loud," he said, pacing a little across the kitchen floor. Lenore began in her polished voice:

> *Miss Angie Carlson:*
>
> *I'm grateful for your kind thoughts and for the lovely gift you brought. You're a sweet child, and I'm so glad Jennifer has a friend such as you. I must tell you about my son. Yes, he is here at Pinewood Acres, and he's determined to have this place for his own. If he has his way, I'll be committed or something, and everything I have will be gone. I'm going away for a few days. You mustn't worry about me. Lenore, my trusted companion, will see to my*

affairs. It grieves me to think that my own son . . . never mind. Thank you again for your kindness to a lonely old woman.

Sincerely,
R. Mara

Harry pursed his lips and pondered the letter silently. Yes, that's good. There would be no need for further visits since Angie would think Rena was away, and seeds of doubt would be planted as to Ogden's motives. Good. Yes. He took the letter and tucked it in his pocket.

"What are you going to do with it?" Lenore asked, staring into his face.

"I'm going to deliver it, my dear. What else?" With that he moved to the door.

"Oh, Harry, are you sure? What if. . . ." Lenore put both arms up and clutched the lapels of his suit.

"Don't worry," he said, his irritation now mixing with the sudden familiar desire that her perfumed nearness often worked on him. "Soon all this will be over, and we'll have the rest of our lives to spend the money." He drew her close and kissed her lips that tasted like the cranberry tonic she had been drinking.

"Oh, Harry. Can we go away soon?"

"Soon," he said with whispered vehemence and passed quietly out the door.

He whisked away from the house through the woods as the dogs began to whine and pace in their pen. He breathed in deeply but felt unrefreshed and heavy with the weight of the letter in his pocket and the burden of his lust.

He had grown familiar with this path, having often

had reason for surreptitious visits to confer with Lenore. He smiled a little to himself. He didn't like it here, this podunk out in the middle of the country, a place crawling with tourists. He'd be glad to get out of here, back to the city and to the night life to which he had grown accustomed.

The main parking lot and the rows of cabins came into view. He reached into his pocket and drew out his little book that he kept for notes. There he had recorded Ogden's license number. Carefully he checked the cars, finding only three of the type Ogden drove. But none had the correct license number. Ogden had gone somewhere! Riggs felt a little panic rise in his throat. Had he gone to the police? Or . . . ?

Easy, man, he told himself, you're reaching. Just because a man's gone off for a late night drive . . . maybe even took some girl with him. Angie? He walked the length and breadth of the lot again and satisfied himself that he hadn't missed the car. Then he crept along the path toward the cabins. He knew which one was hers.

The noises of nature made him nervous, especially at night. It was as though all the trees had eyes and the owls and insects had voices that threatened and taunted him.

"It's your conscience, dear heart," Lenore had teased him once when he had mentioned the noises he disliked so much. She had laughed at him then.

"Lucky I have you to be my conscience, aye?" he had said sarcastically. "Doubly poor I am in that case."

When he had started as manager, he had planned to work nine to five, only lifting off a little cream now and then, taking only his due. Life had milked him until he was dry and empty. He'd never gotten a break in his whole life. But then the idea had come to him, almost like a vision. And the more he had hung around and had put up with that washed-up old woman, the more he had felt justified. It was as though life had finally smiled on him.

He paused a few cabins away from number 25, Angie Carlson's. The wind came up, and he shivered in his summer suit. The wind ruffled his hair and pressed his shirt against his skin, almost like some ill omen borne on the air. He wasn't going to let Richard Ogden or this little Victorian do-gooder spoil things now. He had to stop them. He'd do what he had to.

With surprising agility and silent steps he slipped the letter Lenore had written under Angie's door. Barely a sound came as the paper slid through. Then he quickly walked on, feeling a kind of exhilaration, as though he'd done something very brave and expected to be rewarded.

He whistled under his breath as he walked the rest of the way to his quarters at the other end of the resort. By whistling he could shut out the night sounds that irritated him so much. And as he walked, he defied the wind, willing himself warm in spite of it and suppressing it the way he had always suppressed his stricken conscience, until now it was a thing to laugh at. And laugh he did. The wind carried his hollow little mirth to some secret place in the realm of shadows.

twelve

Sad storms whose tears are vain,
Bare woods whose branches stain
Deep caves and dreary main,—
Wail for the world's wrong!

PERCY BYSSHE SHELLEY

Angie frowned through the cabin window. Last night's wind that had waked her in the early hours had ushered in sullenness and a pouting rain. Leaves had been blown up under the screen door and had swept into the little porch, leaving the corners cluttered with soggy leaves.

She had tried all morning to keep her mind on her reading and correspondence as the rain drummed mournfully on the wooden roof. But she was troubled over Rena and the discovery that she had made yesterday when she had gone to visit Rena. Could what she had said about Richard possibly be true?

Her friendship with Richard had given this vacation special significance. He had become part of the idyllic beauty, the peace, of Pinewood Acres. She didn't want to admit to herself that it could be much more than that. The warning flags had been raised, and she had guarded her heart, to the extent that she had all but told him that she wouldn't see him again. Then yesterday she had learned the disturbing news.

She had made several visits to Jen's Aunt Rena, and each time Angie's feelings for her deepened. She found herself caring about the troubled woman in a way that both bewildered and irritated her. She hadn't wanted to be counselor or helper to anyone on this vacation; she had wanted only to enjoy the peace of untroubled days. But yesterday's disturbing events had changed all that. Staring vacantly at the trembling willow, heavy with rain, Angie tried to piece together the events of that visit.

When she had arrived at the stone mansion, Lenore had made no move to invite her in but had stood facing Angie on the wide veranda with her arms folded, wearing sleek black pants, a green silk blouse, and a broad golden sash, almost like wings. In the pale light she appeared enormously tall and beautifully severe. Angie was astounded by a sudden reminiscence of the beautiful butterfly of her dream, the formidable creature that had lured the little Eddies to the brink of the abyss.

She drew herself back to reality and insisted on seeing Rena. Only after considerable demanding was she ushered grudgingly into the library where she waited nearly a half an hour before Rena appeared.

When the owner of Pinewood Acres did enter the library with Lenore following, she was sober and more energetic than Angie had ever known her to be. She was wearing a cotton housedress of pale blue with small white flowers on the fabric. Her hair, neatly combed and held in place with translucent combs gave her the look of an organized homemaker having completed her housework and about to take a cup of tea. But Angie immediately saw that the amber glass in her hand held something other than tea.

"Are you quite sure you're up to—" Lenore began,

standing aside and watching Rena through those emerald-colored eyes.

"Up to what? Seeing guests in my own home?" came the quick response. Instantly penitent, she said, "Forgive me, Lenore. We'll just have a nice visit here." She set the glass down on a fragile carved table and gave a small shake of her head as Lenore moved away, leaving the door ajar.

The library was a small, spare room with a love seat and two straight chairs. The hardwood floor was clean but unpolished, and the drapes had yellowed in stripes that corresponded to their beige folds. Only the presence of multicolored books gracing all four walls gave the room any sense of comfort.

"I'm afraid I don't read much anymore, but these books have been with me a long time. They were my father's."

Rena sat somewhat heavily on the little couch, a pained expression softening her handsome features. She was silent a long time as her eyes wandered in pale nostalgia along the rows of books. Her lips, bright with pink lipstick, twitched now and then, as though some half gentle memory filtered through her mind. Then she turned her eyes on Angie.

"So, have you any more news from my niece?" she asked quietly.

"Nothing more, just that her father is much improved. Jen is hoping to return soon. I'm sure she'll have good news to share with you when she does."

"And you, my dear, you'll soon be going away. Back home?"

Angie looked away and toyed with a speck of lint on her jeans. "Yes, I suppose. . . ." She paused and then was strangely compelled to talk about her fear, her failure. "I, that is, I'm not sure I will return at all."

Rena cocked her head to one side. "Not return to your job at the mission?" she asked in surprise. You've told me so much about the people there that I feel that I almost know them." She smiled a little and waited for Angie to continue.

"I never told you about Eddie, did I? I mean, how he was killed?" She didn't wait for an answer. "He was murdered—by a child. Another child!" Angie's voice trembled. "Roslyn, his sister, wouldn't cry at the funeral . . . she just sat there with those eyes black with mascara and nothing moving in her whole body. I'd never been able to reach her before, and certainly not then. I don't know, Rena. I just don't know what good I can do . . . for her or for the others." She stopped and cleared her throat, realizing how strange it was that she should be discussing her inner pain with this woman who was unable to help even herself.

Rena seemed deep in thought for a few seconds. Then she lifted those liquid eyes of hers and seemed to fix her gaze on some inscrutable object too grand to be seen. When she spoke her voice seemed different, almost not her own. "Seems to me, if you don't mind my saying so, that you're putting all the burden on one small pair of shoulders. Doesn't leave much for God to do. Funny. And it's His work after all, isn't it?"

Angie remained silent while these words sank deep into her soul. Long afterwards she was to recall them and to dwell upon them, unable to stop thinking of them. Then she smiled. "I'm sorry to bother you with my troubles, Mrs. Mara."

"Call me Rena, dear. I never liked my second husband's name, God rest his soul." She put a hand to her hair, which glowed like copper in the afternoon sun. In the process the lock of hair fell over her left eye, and almost as if by signal, Rena became the childish, vulnerable woman Angie had first met.

"Good news seldom comes to me. Doesn't know my address, I guess," Rena said, pursing those pink lips. She gave a low sigh. "Look at this place. It needs new furnishings, new carpet. It used to be so elegant. Well, the winds of fate, I suppose."

"It seems like such a beautiful resort with so many guests," Angie began. "It gives every evidence of being a flourishing business."

Rena sighed. "Yes, well, one would think so. But we've been losing ground steadily. In the last five years profits have fallen off to the extent that . . . well, forgive me, Angie, I don't want to bore you with these depressing details."

"But really, I—"

"I used to be quite an entertainer, you know, in the old days. Why, people would give their eye teeth to come to one of Rena Ogden's parties." A bright flush came to the woman's pallid cheeks, and her blue eyes took on a youthful glow.

Angie was touched by the beauty of Rena's face. Something gentle, almost kindly, transformed her manner.

"Father used to tell me that I could charm a weasel out of its hole and make a mink give up its stole." She launched into the story of her first business venture, and a freshness, a gaiety, seemed to change her.

Angie listened, aware she was not paying strict

attention. What name had Rena said? Ogden? Strange, that was Richard's last name. But she was quickly engaged by Rena's charming rendition of a once-happier time. Angie also noticed that the glass near her hand had not been touched since she had begun talking with her.

As abruptly as the stories had begun, they ended, as though a book had been suddenly closed. A long silence ensued, and Angie began to feel uncomfortable. She wondered if she should leave, or perhaps see if Lenore had the tea ready.

"I've heard the song before, you know," Rena said suddenly, as though they had been discussing something quite different.

"The song?" Angie asked softly.

"The one the music box plays." The light and color vanished. Only the childish dreaming quality remained. "My mother used to sing it a long time ago. She sang it to me, and I believed that it was really true."

Angie reached across the little space between her chair and Rena's, and she placed a hand gently on the older woman's arm. "It is true. He does love you, you know."

Rena looked directly at Angie then, as though seeing her for the very first time, as though their earlier conversation had not happened.

"I knew you believed that the first time we met. Isn't it funny how you instantly know something about a person?" She paused and harked back to the point of the discussion. "Of course, I don't believe it anymore. Not for me. Not after—"

Angie smiled. "But, don't you see, God's love doesn't depend on what we do or don't do. We can't stop God from loving us. His love isn't like ours, or like any human love. He keeps right on waiting for us, asking us to let Him love us."

Rena Mara rose from the couch, and something stiff and cold seemed to affect her. She walked uneasily toward the window, then turned back again. "I'm going to lose it all, you know," she said, with crisp, even syllables. "And he's already here to pick up the pieces."

"What do you mean, Rena? Who's here?"

"Him. My son. Even my son can't love me. Why should he? Why should anyone?"

Angie watched her incredulously. "Your son is here, at Pinewood?"

"Yes, after all these years of silence he's here pretending to be concerned about his poor old drunken mother, now that I've nearly lost everything. Well, let him have it."

"But Rena, how can you be sure this is so? Maybe he really—"

"Oh, Richard is a sly one. Why would he ignore me for all these years and then come around here and pretend to want to help me save the resort?"

Richard. Richard Ogden! Suddenly Angie felt as though she'd been slapped hard in the face. She held her breath, staring at Rena, everything within her revolting. It couldn't be true. They had talked about Rena and about Jen and Richard had never said a word. He would have told her. Surely he would have told her. Unless. . . .

"Now, there I've spoiled something again. I've upset you," Rena said, murmuring like a penitent child. "I'm sorry to go on so about my troubles."

Angie dug her fingers into the arms of the chair and set her jaw with determination. Rena had her glass in hand

and quickly downed its contents. The blue, blue eyes, so very much like Richard's, Angie now realized, fluttered, then closed with resignation.

"I won't blame you if you go now." She paused. "Really, I'm quite tired anyway."

Angie stood and steeled herself against the impulse to run. But something took hold inside. Some great pity welled up in her heart as she watched the woman, the woman too young to be so old and so betrayed! In a flash all the evils of the world were unmasked and stood glaring at her. Well, they would not destroy this victim!

She dropped down on the little couch and motioned for Rena to sit down. She closed both arms around Rena, who was now shuddering, and drawing in short, shallow breaths like a child inwardly uncomforted.

"Yes," said Angie. "I must go now, but I'll be back. I'm going to help you, Rena. You're not going to lose everything!"

With that she let herself out of the room, pausing only momentarily to frown into the face of Lenore, who had obviously been listening at the door, hearing every word. A look of dark pleasure clouded her features. Angie scrambled down the veranda stairs, her feet as soundless as little rushes of wind in the dying daylight.

She slept little that night, going over and over what Rena had said and trying to remember every conversation with Richard. Had he given any clues that would support Rena's claim? He couldn't really betray his own mother, could he? He was so kind, so good, really. But who could see into the heart of another?

That had all happened yesterday. Now as she opened

the cabin door in the late afternoon, the rain had halted its dismal dripping, as though, like a spent maiden, there were no tears left. She had made little progress sorting out events. Even her decision to phone Richard's cabin and confront him with Rena's claim had come to nothing, for the phone went unanswered. She stared gloomily at the clutter from the wind and rain, thinking she should sweep off the porch.

Instead she put on her sweater and sandals to head for the mansion on the hill. She'd have another talk with Rena. She had to do something. She left the cabin and walked along the road. The woods would probably be too wet, although she longed for the peace and solace of the trees and the little stream that wound through it.

When she arrived at Rena's house, the place was dark except for a porch light shimmering weakly in the dusk. Angie pounded on the door, calling over the bellowing of the dogs as they paced inside their pen, but there was no response at all. This is strange, Angie thought. Rena seldom went out. But perhaps it was not so strange. Maybe Lenore had taken her for a drive or something. Disappointed, she turned back, surprised at how quickly the afternoon had disappeared. Despite the wet ground, she decided to take the shortcut through the woods to return to her cabin. The seclusion and serenity of the forest beckoned her.

She remembered the way, and she stepped down to the little path, picking her way among the clumps of brush and rock. Soon she would be at the stream; even now she could hear its faint trickling sounds. Once over the bridge, there would be little to concern her, although she tried not to think of the rickety planks that formed the old bridge and the sharp jagged rocks at the middle of the stream.

Rena's bitter accusations against Richard rang in her mind. Could he be the plotting, vindictive person Rena thought he was? He was her own son, after all, Angie reasoned. But if she hadn't seen him since he was a boy, who could tell what he might have become?

She recalled the day when the storm had rolled in, how he had gently helped her to safety and had built a roaring fire in the cabin. They had sat together, warm and comfortable with each other. And they had had a beautiful day at the balloon fair, his arm around her shoulders, his warm, wonderful smile!

She shuddered at the surprising coldness of the wind. Clammy weeds clung to her ankles. As she made her way along the path she remembered how Richard had discouraged her from getting involved with Rena. Why? Why hadn't he told her who Rena was?

Somewhere an owl hooted, a mournful, sardonic call. Silvery flashes of moonlight penetrating the tangled screen of trees made quick lightning patterns on the ground, like psychedelic lights twisting in some brothel. Fear clutched her heart as she neared the bridge. Why had she foolishly come this way instead of the safe, well-lighted road?

Suddenly there was a scraping of branches behind her. Silvery light flashing through the foliage joined with quick movements and something blue and white in the bushes. Someone was there! Was he following her? Oh, my God!

Poised like a deer ready to spring away, she peered into the bushes and saw unmistakably someone in a tweed jacket—a striking tan and gold and cocoa tweed like the one Richard wore!

Whirling around, Angie flung herself across the bridge, tearing her hands on the rough railing as she scrambled to steady herself. The heel of her left sandal suddenly caught in the planks and she stumbled to the rough, wet boards.

Tearing her shoe off, she scrambled away from the bridge, on past the arch of pines where once she had enjoyed idyllic moments, and down to the little pathway along the golf course. She couldn't bear to look behind her to see if her pursuer were still coming. With her pulse throbbing, she raced along the ridge, jogged westward to the rows of cabins and, once inside her own shelter, leaned panting against the locked door.

thirteen

Faithful are the wounds of a friend;
but the kisses of an enemy are deceitful.
PROVERBS 27:6, KJV

Rena Mara sat on the edge of the bed and watched night fall. A dismal rain streaked the window and collected in the corners, then fell quietly away. She stared vacantly into the gathering darkness and felt the years collect like rain in the corners of her memory and fall away.

The rain, with its subtle sadness and mystery, had always intrigued her. As a child she had ventured barefoot onto the soggy grass and, laughing for the pure enjoyment of it, had let the cold drops strike her skin and soak her hair and clothes. Now she shivered and drew her sweater close around her shoulders.

It was a child's reminiscence, and she was old now. She wrapped her arms around herself and rocked a little back and forth, sensing a dull ache in her left arm and that stronger ache that could only be relieved by a drink. Just a small one to stop the hurt. But as she reached for the familiar knob, her hand brushed something on the top of the cupboard.

Music . . . the tinkling strains of the song that belonged with rain and barefoot walks and children's dreams. "Jesus loves me, this I know." The notes played slowly, unsteadily, then stopped as the spring was spent. Rena stared at the little ceramic statue of mother and child and traced her fingers over its smooth lines.

"He does love you, you know," Angie had said just yesterday as they sat and talked together. She had wanted to believe the child's words. What a sweet, caring girl she was, so full of natural kindness that she seemed to be a part of some other world. But she too had been wounded. She had tasted the bitterness of life.

"I don't know what good I can do her, or anyone else," Angie had said yesterday, and her eyes had filled with tears.

It was too sad. The longing for a drink plagued her again, but she struggled to repress it. She needed to think clearly for just a little while.

Perhaps she should reconsider Riggs's offer to buy the resort. It was too big for her now, and she was too old. Her touch was gone. She looked around at the dingy room that had once been so charming and well cared for. She had no money for repairs or to purchase new furnishings. It wasn't like the old days. Things cost so much. Riggs had said so. Lenore often reminded her of how much her liquor cost, as though it were her fault that the resort was in the red. What puzzled her was why Riggs stayed on.

Or was he hoping that she'd give in and sell? Rena wondered. But he hadn't mentioned selling again after she'd turned him down the first time. He had merely shrugged and turned away. Lenore had stayed too, and initially Rena had thought that she did so out of loyalty to her. She had enjoyed thinking that. But Lenore was thick with Riggs; no doubt it was on his account that she didn't leave.

Rena listened sadly to a distant rolling of thunder, and it seemed to her like the rolling away of youth and love, mocking her. She was tired, so tired.

She had been happy here at first; she had worked very hard to make this place the finest, and it had been. Papa would have been proud of her. And Richard? She had dreamed of his returning, of being able to show him how well she had done without anyone's help or love, not her husband's, not his. She'd hold her head up high and nod as he exclaimed over the extraordinary features of the resort.

But loneliness is stronger than pride. It saps the strength and dulls the nerve. One day he'll come. He hasn't really forgotten you. She had said these things to herself in days gone by and had held on to her hope. But silence had stretched over the days and years, and hope had died like a flame in the wind.

Perhaps it was time to sell out. What did she need with a big house and a business? She could move into town, find a comfortable apartment and have the money she needed to buy. . . . But she didn't want to finish the thought.

It wasn't true, was it? She could live without it. To prove it to herself she moved away from the cupboard and dressed carefully in a royal blue satin caftan with tiny buttons at the sleeves and throat.

She brushed her long red hair and piled it on her head. Her head ached, and she wondered briefly if the heavy locks of hair contributed to those frequent pains. Maybe she should cut it. It was out of fashion, after all, and Papa, who had disliked short hair, couldn't complain anymore. At the thought of her father the longing for a drink recurred. But stoically she continued to dress, fastening a single strand of pearls around her neck. She considered her reflection in the smoky mirror.

"Your looks are a great asset, Rena," her father had often said, surveying her as though she were a piece of property to be assayed. "Use everything to your advantage, everything."

She remembered his brilliant, proud eye and the firm grasp of his hands on her shoulders when he had wanted to bring home a point. She hadn't cared for prosperity or acclaim. She had only wanted him to hold her and tell her that he loved her—Rena—for herself, to tell her he was proud of her whether she became rich and famous or not. But he hadn't done that. Oh, why couldn't he have done that? Even once? If he had, maybe she wouldn't have become . . . .

She turned away and hurried from the room, for the urge to drink was almost too strong now for resistance. She closed the door quietly behind her and started down the long staircase. In a moment she realized that she had forgotten to put on her shoes. But the former highly polished floor posed little threat now in its dull state; she wouldn't fall.

Soundlessly she approached the once gracious parlor where she had entertained her business friends and acquaintances and where grand parties had been held. She had been highly regarded as a woman of significance, a business leader to be respected. In her mind's ear she could still hear the tinkle of fine crystal, the polished conversations seasoned with polite laughter.

She spun around once gently, feeling only slightly dizzy. What days those had been! What busy, whirling, teeming days! That's the way it should be. Life should be too full for wondering about motivations or love or the lack of it, too busy to leave time to think thoughts too sad for reflection.

"Don't you see? God's love doesn't depend on what we do or don't do. We can't stop God from loving us . . . not like human love . . . He keeps on waiting for us." Angie's message came back to her in a strange whirl of memory, like an arrow finding its mark. There had never been time for God in her life either. Maybe that had been her mistake.

"Don't be a fool!" The words hung on the air in strange midsentence. But Rena recognized that the words were not in her mind. Someone had really spoken them, a female's voice on the other side of the closed parlor door with its old-fashioned paneled squares of glass.

Rena drew trembling fingers to her lips and leaned close to listen.

"We've got to do something before they ruin everything." It was Harrington Riggs's clipped, even syllables, accompanied by a dull thud on the coffee table.

"Keep your voice down, for Heaven's sake." Lenore's usually smooth voice was tinged with irritation.

"That big city man, Ogden, pushing his nose in here, asking questions, making demands! I should have let the brutes at him when I caught him snooping around the office!"

Rena swallowed. Richard. They were speaking of Richard, her son. So, he had tangled with Riggs. She liked the thought of Riggs standing up for her, protecting her property. Even though she didn't like him and he wasn't much of a manager, he saw to things and kept outsiders away.

Rena leaned against the wall and listened. What had

Richard been doing around the office? And who were "they"?

"Do you think he found anything?" Lenore was asking with agitation.

A sarcastic grunt followed. "What's to find? I cover myself pretty good. Besides, the guy's an amateur. He even left his jacket behind. I could have called the police and had him arrested for breaking and entering."

Police? Breaking and entering? Rena's confusion deepened.

"Calling the police would not have been your most brilliant idea," came Lenore's abrupt response.

"Don't worry. I won't need to call anyone. As long as the old girl won't listen to him, it doesn't matter. And she's so sopped most of the time that she doesn't know which end is up."

"Still, I'd feel better if we just left now. We have enough." Lenore's voice took on a pleading note.

"I've decided that we don't have enough. We're going to get her to sign the deed. The way she thinks things are going she'd be a fool not to dump this place! I think it's time to make her another offer, but not nearly as handsome an offer as my first on. After all, look at how the place has deteriorated." Harry gave a little mirthless laugh.

Sickened, Rena felt herself falter as she leaned against the wall. When a person suddenly recognizes that she has been a total fool, that she's been betrayed by those she thought were her friends, the blow comes like a punch in the stomach and sends her reeling, breathless, and feeling used. What did they mean by having enough now? She tried to focus on their continuing conversation.

"I think they're in on it together, Ogden and that little missionary friend of Jennifer's." Riggs made a low sound in his throat, and his fist made contact with the coffee table again.

In on what? Rena tried to picture Angie and Richard snooping about the office after dark, holding clandestine meetings, and maybe discussing ways to trick her out of her life's savings. But instinctively she knew that Angie was not capable of that. And Richard? In her heart of hearts she couldn't bring herself to believe it. What was Riggs saying now?

"I think I scared her off good, though. When she came here yesterday, I followed her. I put the guy's jacket on and gave her a good scare in the woods. Bet she'll be packing and quickly gone. She won't trust Ogden now either, I'll wager."

"I heard Rena tell the girl herself that Richard was no good, that he was only after her money." There was a ripple of pleasure that was as close as Lenore ever came to laughter. "That girl is so naive, she squeaks. She's got some fool notion about helping."

Rena tightened her grip on the railing. Tears threatened and the sick feeling in her stomach grew. If she could only have a drink!

"She's so sopped most of the time." Riggs's denunciation rang in her ears.

It was true. She had turned into a useless, drunken, old woman. It was the first time that she had allowed the words to complete themselves in her mind. And as she did so, she was filled with a deep self-loathing. It wasn't her father's lack of love, her son's rejection, or anything else that made her what she was. She herself had done it!

There was a rustling of paper and glasses, then footsteps, and Rena knew that they were coming. She tried to hurry back upstairs, but her foot slipped on the stair. She grabbed the railing to avoid toppling to the bottom. If she could just keep her head up and keep from being really sick!

"Rena!" Lenore gave a gasp as she opened the door and exchanged a stricken look with Riggs. "What are you doing here?"

Rena pulled herself up with a masterful effort. "I live here. This is my house," she said with forced dignity.

"Of course, dear," Lenore said, dripping with sincerity. "I only meant . . . why, you've forgotten your shoes! You'll catch cold."

Riggs stood in the hall, hands on his hips, looking like a fat walrus that couldn't choose between squatting on a rock or dropping into the sea. Doubtless he was wondering how much she had heard and how much of what she heard she had understood, Rena surmised. His eyebrows formed a straight line over his dark eyes.

"You don't look well enough to be out of bed, Mrs. Mara," Riggs said, the red flush creeping up his thick neck.

"Your concern for my health is quite touching," she said icily. It was a mistake, she knew instantly. Lenore and Harry exchanged troubled but transparent glances, obviously recognizing that at least part of their conversation had been overheard.

"Are you going somewhere? You must rest and let us take care of these business details," Lenore said, lifting her chin in a cultured, professional way. There was a dangerous edge to her voice that made Rena go cold.

Rena started slowly up the stairs. She felt the strange need to keep swallowing, and her breath came in difficult gasps. Fear. It was the first time she had really been afraid of Lenore and Riggs. How far would these two go in their hunger for money? She recalled parts of the conversation: Angie, the jacket, and the woods. She wavered on the stair.

"Here, let me help you," Lenore said, slipping a satiny arm around her, which to Rena had the decided effect of a snake coiling itself around her ribs.

"Get her a drink!" Riggs muttered with disgust.

Lenore half pushed, half prodded her the rest of the way and into her room. Rena allowed herself to be helped to the bed and she sat there, shuddering inwardly, afraid to look at Lenore. With perfectly controlled motions Lenore poured an enticing liquid into a crystal glass.

"Sleep now. You'll feel much better in the morning," Lenore purred.

She hated herself for it but, with trembling fingers, she put the glass to her lips. Lenore passed her with a little rush of wind and left the room. As Rena took the first swallow she heard the key click in the lock. Lenore had locked the door from the outside.

fourteen

> Greatly his foes he dreads, but more his friends;
> He hurts me most who lavishly commends.
>
> CHARLES CHURCHILL

Angie woke with a start and listened to the soft crying of rain against the window. The sky, the rocky bluff, and the tree-covered plain all united in one gray, inconsolable wash of pity.

Her sleep had been fitful. The scratches on the heel of her left hand ached insistently now, as though urging her to wake and remember. Remember Rena with her languid face, the eyes that shone with familiar blue clarity. Remember Richard's name falling with bitterness from the pouting lips. And remember the fear, salty and choking, as she scrambled over the broken planks of the bridge, thick with vines and tangled branches. Remember the tweed coat, his coat.

She sat up, braced herself against the raised pillows, and watched the gray panorama as though it could give some clue to the distortion of events. It was no clearer now than during the long hours of darkness after her flight through the woods to her cabin. No one had appeared or called or threatened. Perhaps the whole thing was in her imagination: the crunching of leaves, the feeling of being observed, the eerie pursuit.

But there could be no denying that someone had been there, watching her as she made her way back from the stone mansion. That person had been wearing Richard's tweed jacket, the same handsome coat against which she had laid her cheek when they had drifted in timeless serenity in the magical balloon.

Her mind lingered over every conversation, every look and touch. Rain. It had rained on the day they had first met on the high outcropping of rocks, when they had run to her cabin for shelter and shared coffee in front of the fire . . . those first few moments of getting to know one another. She could never have thought that this could be the same man who had left his mother to drink away her life and who had returned not to give to but to take from her the only thing she had left.

Perhaps the whole thing was some dreadful mistake. Maybe . . . maybe what? No plausible explanation formed, only that gnawing question mark that coils itself around the stomach and ends with one sharp punch.

She got up and splashed water into the tea kettle. What a mess she'd made of the whole thing. She should have left Jen's message with Rena Mara that first day and let it go at that. Instead she and Rena had become friends. Now her friend was in trouble. But she had not been able to help. Even as her efforts to help Eddie, Roslyn, Jake, and the others had failed, this attempt to lift Jen's unhappy aunt had likewise resulted in dismal failure.

"Doesn't leave much for God to do. Funny. And it's His work after all, isn't it?" Rena's words, spoken as she fixed those blue eyes on some unknown object, came clearly to Angie now.

She had unburdened herself to Rena as they had sat together in the library of the mansion. Angie had told her that she might not return to the mission after all. She had described Eddie's desperate little life snuffed so early and the despair of his older sister who had loved him so much. She hadn't meant to talk about that, not to Rena who had so much trouble of her own. And yet. . . .

Had God chosen Rena as His instrument for disseminating truth? Hadn't He chosen a pagan Persian king to bring about the return of His people to their land? God's messengers were often unlikely harbingers of truth. She puzzled over the possibility now. Rena's words had struck a reminiscent note. Loving and lifting people was indeed God's work; it remained for His people simply to be faithful, to do as He directed, and to leave the results with Him. She had always known this. And yet, had she lost sight of that important concept?

The sharp whistle of the tea kettle brought her focus back to the present. Her failure one way or another was not the issue here. Rena was losing the resort for which she'd worked so long and hard. She had already lost a husband . . . and a son. Her health was draining away, and no one seemed to care what happened to her.

Oh, it was all so absurd, this questioning, wondering, fearing. Angie knew the Lord's way well enough; the Scriptures taught it plainly. She would simply confront Richard with Rena's accusations and fears. She would discuss with him his relationship to Rena. If there were an explanation for his behavior, he'd have a chance to share it. The truth, straightforward and unswerving, was needed here. Her telephone calls to Richard's cabin went unanswered. But she must find a way to meet with him. Perhaps she'd leave a message at the resort office.

She showered and dressed in warm slacks and a cotton shirt the color of cornflowers. After a cup of tea she grabbed her raincoat and left her cabin, locking it for the first time since she had come to the resort. As she stepped out onto the little screened-in porch she gave a casual kick at a clump of leafy debris that had collected near the screen door and suddenly spotted an envelope.

The sealed envelope was blank except for the wet stains and dirt. Curiously she opened it, and read the strange lines in a halting feminine hand.

Angie stood for some time with the letter in her hand, turning it over and over, as though it would give her answers to the many questions flooding her mind. So Rena had gone away somewhere! That's why the place was so quiet last night. She must have left shortly after Angie's last visit with her, when she had learned the truth about Richard's identity. But where would Rena go? And how could Richard take the resort from her? Where was Richard?

As Angie moved slowly away from her cabin, the air was heavy with the scent of honeysuckle and foxglove, but she found little enjoyment in it, only sensing a dull distaste like the smell of food to someone whose appetite has slackened.

She headed for the resort office. Lenore, "trusted companion," would be the one to ask, if she too hadn't dropped off the face of the earth! Feeling forlorn and alone Angie approached the office where marigolds stuck out in garish profusion in the somber morning.

Although it was not early, most vacationers were still snuggled inside warm cabins waiting for the rain to subside. There was little activity around the office. She stepped in and was met at the desk by the pudgy, balding man they called Tinker, the same man who had come with Jen's urgent phone message more than a week ago. Angie decided to ask for Richard first. Perhaps the little man knew something of his whereabouts.

"Help you, lady?" he asked, his small eyes lit with the look of a man intrigued with a sense of his own importance. Uneven yellow teeth appeared as he gave a grudging smile.

"I'm looking for a friend. I haven't been able to reach him, but I'd like to leave a message. It's rather important." Angie opened her denim purse to reach for a pencil.

"Name?" he asked.

"Ogden. Richard Ogden."

"Number 7, row C," Tinker said with a pleased grin. "Won't do no good, though." He rocked back and forth on his stocky legs, his hands thrust into his spotty, brown pants.

Angie looked at him, puzzled.

"Saw him light out real late last night, just took off in that blue car of his clean as you please, like it weren't the middle of the night and all."

"Oh, I see." Angie twisted the strap of her purse, wondering what it all meant.

"Reckon he'll be back. Ain't checked out yet," Tinker said, thrusting his tongue against the inside of his cheek and making a crude clicking noise.

Angie hesitated, then pulled a piece of paper from her purse. "Very well. I'll just leave a message in his box. Thank you." She turned and sat down to write, aware of the little man's eyes watching her and hearing his continued funny clicking as though his teeth didn't fit quite right.

She wrote quickly:

Richard,

I must speak with you about a matter of

importance. Please meet me in the coffee shop this evening around six, if you can.

Angie

She folded the note and put it in box C 7, unnerved by the cold little slap of the note as it fell into place in the wooden slot.

"Good Morning, Angie," came a suave, friendly greeting. Harrington Riggs's broad smile and tanned good looks suddenly lit up the darkened room.

"Good morning," she responded lightly, extending her hand.

"I'm glad to see the rain hasn't kept you from coming by. You add a certain charm to this place." He looked at her in a way that made her feel as though he were trying to see inside her. "I certainly hope nothing is wrong. We like to keep our guests happy."

But he didn't give Angie a chance to respond to that last comment. "How about a cup of coffee?" He put his hand on her shoulder and gave it a little squeeze. "It would be a welcome treat for me before tackling the paper jungle in there." He pointed toward his office.

She hesitated. Perhaps she could talk to him about Rena's problem. After all, he was the manager. He would know why things were not going well for the resort. He could shed some light on the situation, couldn't he? Something foreboding nagged at the back of her mind. But surely she could handle his bold approach. "Thanks. I'd like that."

Tinker suddenly called from across the room. "Don't forget about that staff meeting tonight at eight. You told me to make sure everyone was reminded. Reckon that meant you, too."

"It's on my calendar, Tinker," Riggs said rather coldly, then quickly smiled as he ushered Angie into a booth in the coffee shop.

He chattered on as the waitress brought coffee and cheese Danish pastries and set them down with a quick flutter of her red-tipped nails. "How did you enjoy the balloon fair?" he asked, biting into a pastry with relish.

Surprised, she looked up. Since when were her private affairs a matter of public knowledge?

"The balloon fair is a good attraction for us here. People come from all over, and a lot of them spend some time here. It's a great event, isn't it?" He munched his pastry and watched her.

"It was very nice," she said without feeling. "Mr. Riggs—Harry—"

"Ah, here it comes," he said with a rush of humor, "the biting complaint."

"No complaint. I was just going to say that I'm really worried about Aunt Rena. Well, that is, she's not really my aunt. My friend, Jen, she's her aunt. But, I've gotten to know her during these days and—"

"Cream? Here's sugar, too." He moved them in front of her and folded his hands to listen in studied interest.

"You see, Aunt Rena is, well, she's so worried and unhappy about how things are going, and that makes her drink more, and . . ." Angie let the words trail off, not sure how to resume.

"Darn shame about Rena," he said, eyes still glued on hers. "Pity. But what can one do?"

"Mr. Riggs—uh, Harry—what exactly is wrong? Why is the resort failing?"

"What gives you that idea?" Riggs asked, pursing his

lips and retaining a deeply innocent look.

"Well, Rena said—and—and Richard told me—that thousands of dollars are being lost annually."

Something cold he could not hide penetrated Riggs's calculating eyes. "Richard? You mean that son of Rena's, the one who split years ago and never gave his mother two cents' worth of his time? I suppose he'd like to get his hands on this place. But Rena's too smart to let that happen." He paused, scratched his chin, and resumed. "But on the other hand, she's not up to handling things here by herself."

"How do you know this, Harry?" she asked. "I mean, that Richard's after the resort?" Why did it hurt so much to hear Richard spoken of this way? Could it possibly be true? But why would Riggs tell her this, if he didn't have some reason?

"Angie, you must realize that Rena is a hopeless alcoholic. Lenore has done everything she could and continues to care for her, but really, if you've any influence with Rena, you should convince her to sell the resort to someone who could handle it. She could live handsomely anywhere she wished and get all the treatment she needed."

Angie watched the muscles in the square, florid face and the pulsing veins in his neck. Was that it? He wanted to buy the place himself? She met his eyes coolly.

"Someone like yourself, perhaps?" she asked.

"I've offered her a very fair price." There was a silence between them and a tension very nearly palpable. Recovering, Riggs flashed his teeth in a gracious smile.

"Well, my dear, it's very nice talking with you, but I must get to work. The jungle awaits." He rose and held out a hand to help her from the booth.

She refused it, pretending to need both hands for her

purse and raincoat, and followed him silently out of the shop and into the lobby. He waited at the door, eyeing her with a mix of curiosity and nonchalance and fell in step beside her.

"Whatever Rena decides, I certainly hope you'll come visit often," Riggs said, open pleasure in his face.

"Harry, where has Rena gone?"

"Gone? Why, I'm sure I don't know." The little veins in his neck were pulsing again.

"Really," she said, suddenly overwhelmed with a sense that something was really wrong here. Should she mention the letter? "But she's not at home. I—"

"Lenore, dear!" Riggs called.

Angie turned to see Lenore approaching, her tall body moving like a swaying reed in the wind. She carried some papers in her hand, and a pencil lay neatly over one ear and protruded through her black coiffure.

"Angie tells me that Rena has gone away. Is there something you haven't told me?" Riggs gave her a mock scolding look.

"Gone away?" she asked with smooth incredulity. "I just came from bringing her breakfast in her room. I'm sure I don't know what Miss Carlson is talking about."

"But—but," Angie began, her mind whirling. "Last night there was no answer when I called."

"Last night, hmm. Ah, yes, I was away for a brief period. I'm so sorry I wasn't there to greet you. Rena goes to bed early and sleeps very heavily these days. But I assure you, she's not planning any trips right now."

Angie felt a cringing in her stomach as she looked from Lenore to Harry. Why would Rena write a note and tell her that she was going away when she wasn't? Had she lost touch with reality? Angie found herself rejecting that possibility. No, Rena Mara was an alcoholic, but she wasn't senile or demented.

She stared at Lenore until the tall woman turned away with a brusque apology about having a great deal to do. But those cold, emerald eyes had pierced Harry's with an inscrutable look of warning.

They were standing just outside Riggs's office. He suddenly broke the silence. "Oh, there goes my phone again. Forgive me, Angie, but I'll have to beg off as well. Do come by anytime. And stop worrying about things that are beyond your control. Go for a swim or play some tennis. Enjoy your vacation."

Angie watched him go into his office, the door to which was partly open. Something caught her eye in the crack between the hinge and the door frame. Someone's coat hung on a hook behind the door and part of the sleeve was lodged in the crack.

The coat was brown and tan tweed with a bit of the elbow patch visible. Suddenly she realized that it was exactly like Richard's coat! But what was it doing here? Was it the same coat that she had seen last night in the woods? There were not many such coats; it was a bit old-fashioned. She had even told Richard that she liked it especially because of its uniqueness.

She turned and left the lobby, the texture and color of the coat burning in her vision and in her heart. The echo of the closing door and the sounds of Lenore's footsteps on the tile gave desolate accompaniment to the vision. And Angie knew she was alone, alone and bewildered in a hall of mirrors where only distortions, no true reflections of truth, existed.

fifteen

Errors like straws upon the surface flow;
He who would search for pearls must dive below.

John Dryden

Angie left the office, her mind whirling with the startling events that continued to unfold, bringing new questions and disturbing puzzles. Rena was gone, or at least she had said so in the note. But Lenore had insisted that she had just served breakfast in bed to her. Richard was gone, no one knew where, and his disposition of the difficulties at Pinewood Acres were in direct opposition to Harrington Riggs's statements.

Rena Mara mistrusted Richard whom she felt was interested only in her money and more particularly in having Pinewood Acres for himself. But Angie had found Richard to be tender, thoughtful, and honorable in every way. If he could just explain that his interests here were not singularly mercenary, as Riggs had indicated. If only he were here to say that his mother's words were not true! But why had he not spoken of his mother? Where could Richard have gone in the middle of the night?

She circled the resort area, ever watchful for Richard's car. She must stay close to the office, for she had asked him to meet her. She wasn't sure how long she walked, finding little joy in the lovely things that usually attracted her to the idyllic surroundings. One image stumbled over the next, dancing to new twists and strange distortions, playing on her mind like frames in a horror movie: Richard in his tweed coat leaping through the forest, chasing her, frightening her away; Lenore, like one of many tall pines shrouded in dark mystery, cold and solemn; Rena, childish and forlorn, like some maiden in a tower deep in the woods, waiting to be rescued.

Yes, Rena was the real victim here. Angie understood that her own relationship with Richard, that Harrington Riggs's true character, and that Lenore's position in this whole thing were secondary and unimportant. Rena was the one whose person and property seemed up for grabs to the most avaricious of those characters. What would happen to her?

Angie sat a long time by the little stream, pondering what she might do to help. In many ways, Rena was a lot like she had been before God's love had settled upon her heart. She too had been fearful, weak, so conscious of human betrayal. Worst of all, she had been without purpose, for the purpose of the victimized is survival, and sometimes revenge.

God had shown her that there was so much more. She had felt her own spirit soar in gratitude, not so much for the pleasures of life and living, but for the awareness that she possessed a remarkable treasure which no one, however greedy or cruel, could take from her. That treasure was God's presence in her life and spirit.

Angie knew that she had lost sight of this most valuable treasure, even in the very act of service to God. She had allowed the failures and the disappointments to blind her to what her life was really about. Strange. She tossed brittle stems of weeds into the stream and watched them float on the surface, intermingling with the sporadic raindrops.

Only He knew the real scheme of things and how each part of His creation fit and balanced. From His creatures He required only faithfulness to what is true and good and lasting. In a way it was Rena who had brought that truth into focus once again.

Angie rose and walked back along the path, circling the little office. She was glad that she had worn her comfortable shoes, for she had walked the afternoon away. The air remained misty and cool, and a cloud cover brought an unnatural darkness. She decided to wait in the coffee shop. Surely Richard would respond to her note soon.

As she entered the lobby Tinker eyed her curiously, but his inquisitiveness kept him from responding openly. He pressed his tongue against the inside of his cheek and scratched his bald head with one pudgy finger.

Inside the coffee shop she took a booth facing the entrance so that she'd be sure not to miss Richard. She ordered a pot of tea and settled down to wait.

There were enough people there to render her anonymous, but not too many to inhibit concentration. She slipped off her raincoat and poured the first of many cups of tea. With each one disappointment mingled with growing concern: there was no sign of Richard. Had he received her note and simply chosen not to come? Or was he still unaware of her message?

"There are so many lonely people in the world and so few who care at all," he had said. Now it seemed long ago. She had been sure that he too was one of those who cared.

There was such sensitivity and depth to Richard. Their conversations had been so meaningful. She had sensed a goodness, an honesty in him that was absent in so many of the men she had met. Could she have been so wrong? Was he not at all what he seemed? Had he so unbalanced her with those clear blue eyes, that winsome smile, that tender attentiveness? It wouldn't be the first time that a woman had mistaken those things and let her heart rule.

O, dear God, help me to know what to do. She cupped her hands around the smooth, warm cup. The amber liquid trembled inside it, and as she stared into its depths it seemed to Angie that all the joy, the anguish, the evil propensity, and the holy shining of humanity shimmered there. Life flowed in the cup.

But was not life in the Father's hands, He who formed it and breathed into it Spirit, His Spirit? Had He not already drunk of that cup—all of it—in order to identify forever with humanity, to establish victory?

Acknowledging her Lord's sovereign power and perfect love brought a deep sense of awe. It was as though His own pierced hands covered hers in that moment. What incredible strength and tenderness! Whatever happened, He was still so wonderfully present, and there was no crisis beyond His power, not even dear, lost Eddie or Roslyn, sad child-woman left behind!

The door opened and closed many times as the minutes marched on. Now it was eight o'clock and still Richard had not come. Angie put on her raincoat, slowly belting it around her waist. Well, if Richard would not talk to her, she would look for answers elsewhere. She would have to look deeper than the surface of the events, errors that seemed to litter the last few days. Somewhere, beneath it all, the real truth lay shimmering like some rare gem.

The plan to revisit the stone mansion had been forming

in her mind all evening. Would Rena be there, as Lenore and Riggs had assured her? She knew that Lenore didn't want her around. That had been clear from the start. But why? And why did Riggs discourage every attempt to approach Rena? What was going on?

She suddenly remembered the staff meeting she had heard Tinker remind Riggs to attend. Yes, Riggs and Lenore would be busy. They needn't know that she mistrusted their characterization of the events and condition at Pinewood Acres, but she must find out for herself if Rena was indeed safe at home. She could go to the house and not be turned away. But suddenly she remembered the dogs! Yes, Riggs and Lenore would be away from the house because of the meeting, but those beasts would be there! And would the door be unlocked?

She ordered two hamburgers to go, barely working out what she would do with them. The thought of those enormous teeth that she had once faced frightened her terribly. Suppose someone else had been left to stay with Rena, someone else to deter visitors? She stuck the paper-wrapped burgers into her denim bag and slipped out of the coffee shop behind two boisterous, pot-bellied men in polo shirts.

It was still raining. Slanting streaks of water fell in unsteady rhythm, as though Nature were unsure how long it would continue its tearful lament. Glad for her flat, comfortable shoes, Angie walked on past the long rows of cottages and the deserted golf course.

Once in the wooded area the ground was a little drier, for it was shielded by the great canopy of trees. She hummed to herself as she walked on, trying not to think about the last time she had taken this path and had been chased in the eerie moonlight. Only when she came to the old wooden bridge did she cease humming to pick her way carefully in concentration. Here she had fallen in her panic and scraped her arm and hand. The moon was still obscured by clouds; the darkness suffocated everything.

She reached the bluff, shivering now, feeling damp clear through. There was the house, bleak but for one light in an upstairs window, Rena's window! Was she home after all? If so, what was the meaning of the letter?

She stopped to test the wind. If she walked around and came up from the east side, her scent would not be so readily carried to the dogs on the damp westerly breeze. The rain would help deflect her presence, too.

She crept along the edge of the clearing until she reached the other side of the mansion. Then slowly she advanced to the house, opening her bag as she went. Keeping her eyes on the sleeping gray hulks in the wire pen, she pulled out the hamburgers. She fumbled to open the wrappings, her fingers stiff from the cold.

She was almost upon the dogs when they became aware of her. Dazed with surprise they rose, growling, nostrils twitching, for they had caught the scent of meat, driving all their senses toward satisfying their aroused hunger.

Quickly she hurled the hamburgers and ran around to the front door as the dogs pursued the projected missiles. By the time they had swallowed the delectable decoys she had tried the front door—it *was* unlocked!—and was quickly inside the house. Only the dogs' restless yammering ensued and quickly abated in the damp evening.

Angie huddled in the dark hallway and waited. She felt her pulse jumping and pounding at her temples as she listened for sounds, but only a grim silence lay deep around her.

A dim light from the living room was enough to make everything quite visible. She stepped into the room where a small table lamp was lit near the gleaming upright piano. A copy of a woman's magazine lay opened on the recliner and a half-filled cup of coffee rested on the floor by the chair. Apart from that, the room was orderly with the false tidiness of disuse.

"Is anyone here?" she called. After all, she had no intention of intruding on someone's privacy. "Aunt Rena!" Then she heard steps from above and a light rattling of a door.

"Aunt Rena. It's me, Angie."

She hesitated at the base of the stairs. But there was no response. She climbed the spiral staircase and moved down the hall in the direction of the woman's room. "Mrs. Mara?" She stopped directly outside the door. The knob moved again, but the door did not open.

"Is that you, Aunt Rena?"

The voice sounded strange, secretive. "Yes, it's me, but I can't open the door. It's locked from the outside."

"What?"

"The door. It's locked from the outside! Quick, look in the middle drawer of the desk in the library. It's where we keep all the keys."

"Okay," Angie whispered, suddenly very frightened. Who had locked Rena in her room? Why? "Are you all right, Aunt Rena?"

"Yes, but hurry."

The keys were in the drawer, as Rena had said. With shaking fingers Angie unlocked the door and stepped quickly in, closing the door behind her.

Rena Mara leaned against the wall near the door. She wore a cotton dress with enormous yellow flowers that seemed to swallow her up. Her hair had slipped from its pins and tumbled around her pale face in startling disarray. Angie put an arm around the trembling shoulders and looked into the anxious eyes.

"What's happened, Aunt Rena? Why are you locked in?"

She only shook her head slightly, as though dazed. "I'm—I'm not sure—only . . . I heard them talking."

"Who?"

"Harry and Lenore." Rena brushed a stray curl back from her forehead and continued, as though thinking it out for herself as well. "I—I hadn't meant to spy on them, but I heard them talking about you and about Richard."

Angie helped her to the bed, for she seemed faint. "Aunt Rena, why did you tell me that you were going away?"

Rena gave her a clouded, helpless look. "Going away?" she repeated blankly. "I didn't tell you I was going away."

"The letter, Aunt Rena. You sent me a letter. I found it under the door today."

Rena shook her head, dazed. "I didn't write to you, Angie. But I'm so glad you're here. I wanted someone to come. I . . . I'm just so . . . tired. I—" She paused. "Angie, dear, I need a little something from my cabinet there. Could you—"

Angie followed her gaze to the liquor cabinet. There was a silence between them as each considered the import of the request. Then Angie sat down next to her on the bed. "Let's talk first. I want to help you. I think that I can help you, if you'll let me." Her words seemed to come from somewhere outside herself, and she was surprised at the strength and assurance she felt.

"No one can help me," Rena whispered hoarsely. Thunder rolled near, and the rain pounded against the roof with new vigor.

"That's nonsense," Angie said firmly, drawing a tissue from the table and handing it to Rena. She watched Rena wipe her eyes and thought again how remarkably like Richard's they were. "Now, tell me who locked you in here."

There was a bitter twist in Rena's reply. "It's for my own good. Lenore said so. After all, I'm a hopeless alcoholic, didn't you know?" She paused as though hearing words she had never before spoken for the first time. "Yes, that's right," she continued, "a hopeless drunk."

"An alcoholic, yes," Angie said quietly, "but not hopeless. Many people have been able to stop the awful cycle you're in now. And they lead productive lives. Nothing is really hopeless as long as there is life. Don't you see, Aunt Rena? God can help you."

A great peal of thunder cut off her words. Then a sound more ominous than any storm's onslaught hurled them both into shocked silence: steps, heavy steps by the bedroom door! The steps stopped. A slow clicking of the lock, steps receding into the distance, and then, before either of them could give voice to their fears, darkness engulfed them.

sixteen

> . . . Leave to the nightingale her shady wood
> A privacy of glorious light is thine,
> Whence thou dost pour upon the world a flood
> Of harmony, with instinct more divine.
>
> WILLIAM WORDSWORTH

"You don't understand, Sergeant. My mother—that is, Mrs. Mara—doesn't realize what's been going on. You see, she isn't well." Richard wearily ran a hand through his sandy hair as he faced the Castor County law official. How was he to tell this story, so much of which was personal and would be tiresome and irrelevant to the man facing him now?

With only casual interest Sergeant Halley thumbed through the sheets of paper Richard had placed on his desk. His mouth, drawn in a contemplative pucker, finally loosened. He leaned back in his chair.

"It does look suspicious, but there's really not much to go on here. Now, if your mother wants to register an official complaint—"

"Sergeant, I'm just asking you to look into the matter. As I said, my mother's not herself these days. She doesn't seem to understand, but I believe that she's being systematically ripped off and that this has been going on for some time. I can't stand by and watch all that she's worked for just handed over to that scheming manager!" Richard knotted his hands in frustration as he rose from his chair.

Sergeant Halley eyed him curiously. Was it in his mind too that what might be worrying Richard was his own inheritance? Perhaps the sergeant believed that all he was being told was colored by self-interest.

"She's alone now, you see, and there's been no one to look out for her. She trusts these people who are running the resort, but her trust is terribly misplaced. I'm really concerned about her." He thrust his hands into his pockets and stepped away.

"You say this has been going on for some time. How is it that you're just now doing something about it? Isn't it a little like trying to close the barn door after the horse is gone?" The sergeant seemed to enjoy his little analogy but quickly sobered. "You think your mother might be in danger from this man, this—"

"Harrington Riggs," Richard supplied. "Will you at least run a check on him, Sergeant?"

His own checking had shown that Riggs might have been arrested for fraud once before in another state. There had been no conviction. An official check might reveal something more.

"We'll see what we can do. But I suggest you have a talk with your mother."

Richard nodded and picked up his raincoat from the chair. Vaguely he wondered what the sergeant would think if he knew about his breaking into Riggs's office. "Here's my card. But I'll be at Pinewood Acres a few more days, at least until I'm sure my mother is safe. I've written that number in. Please call me if you have any information."

"We'll be in touch." Sergeant Halley nodded perfunctorily and abruptly turned to his next item of business.

Richard returned to his car, the dripping atmosphere of the day matching his gloom. It wasn't a refreshing, sweet-smelling shower that washes the world and invigorates the soul; it was an oppressive rain that clogs the lungs and seeps into the corners of the brain like thick fog.

He was tired after the long night of probing and sorting the information gleaned during his midnight raid of Riggs's office. Most of that day he and his staff had checked out the various companies listed in the Pinewood Acres ledgers. The companies *were* bogus; there was no doubt about that. And Riggs had managed to pocket tidy sums, the total value of which was anybody's guess. Nerves ragged, his mind whirling like a tornado bouncing across an open plain, Richard drove in the direction of Pinewood Acres, unsure of what he should do next.

He must make sure that his mother's safety was not in danger, and Angie's, too. Riggs had figured Angie was a fellow snoop. If things were as Richard suspected, Riggs could very well be a danger to Angie. Dark frustration clawed at his mind. He wanted to march in and confront Riggs with the whole scheme, maybe get in a good punch or two. But that would hardly solve anything.

He must not yet force Riggs's hand until the authorities had had time to investigate, if indeed they would do anything. If Riggs got skittish and ran out now, there would be no recourse. And Rena would lose too much.

Late in the afternoon he stopped for a cup of coffee at a small restaurant along the banks of the river. Another hour or so and he would be back at Pinewood Acres. He took a seat near the window and looked out on the gathering gloom. It was a beautiful spot, but the river's gray water with the rain weeping into it brought an inexplicable loneliness to him.

He leaned back wearily against the seat and tried to organize his thoughts. His talk with Rena had been unsuccessful; she hadn't wanted to listen. After all the silent, painful years, she would not believe him. The old bitterness, the rejection, rose inside him. Perhaps some things could not be changed, perhaps they were beyond one's ability to adjust.

A sudden crying near the window startled him. A gull was tearing its way above the tall tops of the pines, as though it had lost its way in the clustered forests of the earth. But it seemed to sense the nearness of the Big Water for which it longed. Yet for some reason it seemed confused and continued to soar, then backtrack, crying again, unable to find rest. Its call echoed in the pounding rhythms of the night and rang in unison with his own hurting spirit.

Strange "prayers," such as he had never heard in church, rose almost apart from himself and yet intrinsically deep within himself until he sensed an inexplicable assurance the he was not struggling alone. The form of God as suffering man filled him with a pulsing conviction until he was so full that his soul could no longer hear the words of the strange prayers. Like the gull sensing the nearness of the Big Water, Richard sensed the nearness of the One for whom he had searched so long.

But how could it be that the sufferings and death of Christ could atone for his sins? Yet, that is what the Scriptures taught. How could one accept a thing like that?

Angie had spoken of it as they soared in the balloon on that blue summer afternoon. She had spoken of God's great love for humanity, a love great enough to bring Him to earth as a man Himself to teach us His way. Richard remembered again the luminous shining of her face and the clear word of faith on her lips.

That was the crux of the thing. It all hinged on that thing called "faith," always such a nebulous concept to him. Was it so for everyone? He had read about Thomas and had understood him so well. What had made Thomas's heart turn toward the Master in spite of his doubting was that he had not been harshly rebuked and turned away because it was so difficult for him to believe. Tender were the Master's words when He told Thomas to reach out his hands and touch Him.

But where are you now, my God? I want to reach out and see the marks in your hands and feet and your side. Richard's unspoken prayer came from the depths of his soul.

The screaming of the confused gull came once again. It still had not found the Big Water, and it was soaring blindly, agonizingly, above the trees, finding no clear, cool place to land. There was only a maze, a tangled, black maze through which the life-giving water could not be seen. But the river that ran to the open sea was just beneath the crying gull. "Drop down, drop down, and you'll be safe, resting on the floating waves," Richard whispered.

He wondered if he were like the gull, soaring above the truth he had read about in the Bible and innately knew but unwilling to drop down, unable to believe that the life-giving water would be there, as the promise was written. He'd read more of the Bible in recent months than he had in his entire life. He'd even recalled its precepts and had tried to live by them. But he had been unable to do so. Must he, like the gull, settle in faith over the great unknowable waters of life, believing in Him who made the waters?

It was a strange setting for such an eternal moment. But Richard's decision was made, and when it was done he lifted his eyes to the heavens. The gull made one more groping circle over the pines and dropped down onto the breast of the river. It wobbled only slightly, head straight ahead, eyes bright as beads, and then rested white and calm on the gray expanse.

Evening had settled when he pulled into the resort. Everything looked much the same, although no one was about. His body ached for sleep, but his mind and heart were alive with a sense of direction and vigor that was exhilarating. There was much to do, so much he wanted to say to his mother. He could do with a shower and a change of clothes, but first he should check his box. There may have been a message.

He smiled briefly at the blond receptionist who looked up as he entered. He wondered where Tinker, the established night clerk, could be. The blond woman replaced the telephone receiver with graceful, purple-tipped fingers and eyed him cautiously, a studied frown on her perfectly matched lips.

Richard gave his cabin number, and even as he did so he saw a small folded piece of paper protruding from his slot. He took the paper from the receptionist, too curious to remember his manners. Abruptly he turned and left the office, reading as he walked back to his car.

A skip in his stomach and a strange foreboding came over him. The note had been written that day. Six o'clock?

It was now nearly nine. He turned back to the office and strode through the double doors, past the wide-eyed receptionist and into the coffee shop. He searched for the familiar delicate form, the light brown hair, the luminous face. But only a burly truck driver bent over his coffee and a young couple sipping sodas populated the little restaurant. He waited a few moments, just in case, but quickly turned away and reapproached the blond receptionist.

"Please. I need Miss Carlson's number. Angie Carlson."

"Oh, I'm sorry, Miss Carlson checked out tonight." Her violet eyes held his in inscrutable innocence. But she had seemed quite ready for the question, quite poised and polite.

"Checked out? But—"

The girl rechecked her register. "Yes, here it is. Angie Carlson. She checked out about seven-thirty this evening."

An incredible sense of loss gripped him as he backed away and stepped into the drizzling evening. She was gone, and without even saying goodbye. But had she tried to say goodbye?

What had he expected? There was no reason to assume she would wait. After all, he had left without telling her where he was going, without telling her how much she meant to him, without telling her how he. . . . Richard caught his lower lip with his teeth. Still, it was strange that she would be gone tonight. He was sure that she had planned to remain another week.

He searched the note again as the feeling of emptiness filled him. *A matter of importance*. It didn't sound like a farewell. What could the matter of importance be? She was gone! And he couldn't even feel grateful that at least she was away from this mess with Rena and Harrington. Oh, Angie!

He stopped at her cabin just to be sure. Perhaps the receptionist had been mistaken. But there was no light, no response to his knock. He was hurt as he recalled the poignant memory of that afternoon when they had raced together to shelter from the sudden storm over the lake. The sweet hurt engulfed him as he thought about the far-flung sky, the nearness of her in the balloon as they had soared wild and free in those timeless moments.

The force of his own disappointment startled him. Could he look back on their days together merely as pleasant interludes, or even as a dream of what might have been? No, he had allowed himself to love her. Now she was gone, and he had no idea of how or where to find her.

Morosely he drove along the road toward the stone mansion. Angie and Rena had become friends. Could he dare to hope that his mother might know how to reach Angie, know why she had gone off so suddenly?

Lenore answered his knock amid the fierce barking of the great dogs. How could a person even think with that racket going on?

"I want to see my mother." That last word on his lips was strange, but it had come quite naturally.

"What? I'm sorry, I can't hear you."

"Rena. I want to speak with Rena. Please. It's important."

"Honcho! Jack!"

The hounds skulked away, whining in protest. Lenore turned to him.

"Rena's not here, Mr. Ogden."

"What do you mean, not here?"

"I mean," Lenore said evenly, "that she is not here. I understand that she's gone to visit a sister whose husband has been ill."

Hardly realizing what he was doing, Richard brushed Lenore aside and pushed his way into the house. "I don't believe you!" He raced past her, up the stairs, and flung open the door to his mother's room.

It was empty; an eerie order prevailed. The bed had been made, its green spread drawn up over sunken pillows. There was no clutter of clothing or paper or liquor.

"She wasn't well enough to take a trip on her own. Where is she?" Richard demanded as he clambered down the stairs to face Lenore again.

"Mr. Ogden, I told you. And I'm not used to being called a liar." Her black brows brooded over her green eyes, the color of the sky just before a violent storm.

"I'm telling you that Rena wouldn't have just gone off. She couldn't have in her condition."

"Perhaps her young guest assisted her," Lenore said with great calm and precision.

Helpless, Richard stared into Lenore's face while every nerve pulsed with indignation and frustration. Their eyes locked and held in a terrible silence. Then, a nameless fear clutching his heart, Richard turned away, leaving the door open behind him.

seventeen

> Truth must dazzle gradually
> or every man be blind.
>
> EMILY DICKINSON

Sudden blackness fell around them like some evil net paralyzing their movement and even their speech. Somewhere a loon cried, as though finding its lake dry and barren, its mate blown away in the wind.

Angie listened intently, expecting that any second the net would be drawn tighter around them. All life seemed suspended during those brief moments following the blackout and the latching of Rena's bedroom door. Now the footsteps outside the door receded, and the silence was total but for a faint whimpering from Rena.

"Oh, you shouldn't have come," Rena murmured. "See what I've gotten you into? Oh!"

"Aunt Rena, please don't cry." What could all this mean? Would Harrington Riggs and Lenore really do this? It was unthinkable. Why was it that when some great evil happens, all prior visions of it in the lives of others faded into oblivion? Only this was real! Her eyes began to accommodate the blackness, and benign moonlight outlined shapes in the room.

"Aunt Rena, we've got to get out of here. Do you think you can walk?" Angie put an arm under the woman's shoulders and lifted her up on the pillows.

"They won't let us get out of here. Oh, why didn't I just let him have the place? Then you wouldn't be in this awful situation."

Angie tested the door, rattling it hard in its frame, but it was bolted securely. The window! But they were on the second floor! She pulled the heavy drape away and peered into the night. Not even a tree close enough!

Rena sat up on the edge of the bed now, shivering even though it was quite warm in the room. "There's an old iron fire escape just to the left. See?" Between quick breaths she whispered, "It's old but it's solid. You could get away."

Angie saw the rusty, winding thing as she pressed her face against the glass. It certainly was a way out. She raised the window cautiously. Could they be waiting and watching from outside? The misty night spilled in, carrying the fragrance of honeysuckle on the rain.

"Angie, what happened in the woods?" Rena asked suddenly, as though some fog had been lifted, revealing a buried thought.

Angie was fumbling through Rena's closet. Rena would need something to keep her warm and dry. She paused at the sudden question. How could she tell Rena that it was probably Richard who had chased her? Even as she thought it, her heart rebelled.

"I heard him say that he scared you terribly. Oh, Angie, you must get away from here as quickly as you can." Rena brushed the falling front lock of hair away and paused again. "It was something about a coat." Rena's hand paused in midair. "But why would Harrington want you to think—"

Angie's heart skipped a beat. She hurried over to sit next to Rena. "Think what, Aunt Rena? Tell me what you heard."

"Well, I think they were talking about Richard—my son—about him spying in the office and leaving his coat behind.

And Harrington said he had used the coat to give you a scare in the woods. Oh, Angie, I'm afraid I was so drunk I didn't make sense out of it. I still don't understand."

But Angie understood enough, and her heart leaped for joy. It hadn't been Richard in the woods at all. It was Riggs, and he had been using the trouble between Richard and his mother. As long as he could keep Rena at odds with her son, he had little to fear from her and could continue to use her and play upon her illness.

"Rena, put this on! And shoes! Do you have some comfortable shoes? We're getting out of here. We'll get to the authorities and—"

"I . . . can't. Don't you see, I can't! You go. You get away."

"I'm not going without you. Now, you can do it." Angie scrambled through the closet and came up with a pair of low-heeled shoes and a warm coat. She brought them to Rena and began to help her get dressed. "We're both going to get out of here, and we're not going to let Harry steal Pinewoods Acres from you. God will help us—together!"

Angie wrapped the coat around Rena's shoulders and closed it over the yellow flowered dress. "Draw the belt. We don't want any excess material to get in the way."

"I just don't think I—"

"You can. You can!" Angie said firmly. Rena's trembling unnerved her, but she helped her into the shoes and kept talking to her with soothing encouragement. Energy born of anger surged through her. Rena was a sick woman who had been denied any real help for far too long. She practically carried Rena to the window.

"I'll go first. Then I can steady your steps from below," Angie told her.

Rena obeyed and miraculously picked her way down the

narrow, thin-railed steps to the ground. A pale glow of moonlight through the eerie clouds shone on the iron steps as Rena stepped to the ground, her hands held fast in Angie's.

Angie tried not to think what—or who—might be waiting to capture them. She concentrated on helping Rena to walk, not trusting even a whisper. She smiled assurance to Rena and laid a finger to her lips.

Grateful for the cover of the woods, Angie led Rena to the thick cluster of trees near the back of the house. Not until they reached the thicket did she think of the great dogs. Somehow the animals had not sensed their presence. Perhaps they were drowsy after their hamburgers from the coffee shop. Thank God!

"Are you all right?" she whispered to Rena, hugging the woman's arm closer to her side as they moved over the soggy ground.

"I think so, but where will we go?"

"To the road. It's not far. Surely someone will come along and we'll get to town. Then we'll—" But Angie hadn't thought beyond that. "We'll just concentrate on getting to the road as quickly as we can."

The clouds obscured the moonlight and the dark closed in around them like a cloak, but there was just enough light to keep them from stumbling. Angie was glad that she had taken other treks through this wood or they might have fallen over one of the many rocks and clumps of tangling brush.

The little creek, sometimes joyous with tiny cascading tunes, sang only of swollen sadness. Angie guided Rena over the far left side of the bridge, remembering the loose plank on the right where she had fallen. She had thought that she was running from Richard with that sick disappointment that clutches closer than fear. But it had really been Harry! She remembered Richard's arms around her as they had talked in the balloon, and the warmth of that remembrance consoled her and energized her.

Before long lights from cars passing on the highway could be seen through the trees, like twinkling lights on a Christmas tree. They were going to make it! Angie felt a quickening joy and even Rena began to breathe easier.

"He came to see me, you know."

"Who, Aunt Rena?"

"My son. I was drunk, drunk and sick in my heart. I asked him to have a drink with me. Can you believe it? My own son. I—"

"Aunt Rena, what happened between you?"

"Oh, it was so long ago. He was such a good child. But I—I was busy making a name for myself . . . and making my daddy proud." The tears mingled with the rain on her face. "I didn't know how to be a mother. I was too much a child myself." She paused, and for a few moments they trudged on toward the road in silence.

"He left me when he turned seventeen and I never saw him again, until he came here. He told me that he wanted to help me. But I know how he must hate me. I accused him of wanting my money."

Angie listened carefully, heard the bitter hurt of Rena's words. What was it about humans that made them such great innovators of technical engineering, such great conquerors of impossible spaces, such masters of everything except of their own impoverished selves? What was it that kept them broken and separated from each other?

She knew, of course. Without God, man was master of nothing and slave to everything. All that really mattered in life was held in Him. Without Him life was torn to tatters and tossed to untamed winds. Such was the condition of Rena's life.

Richard hate his mother? Surely not the Richard she had come to know. "Oh, Aunt Rena. I don't think it's true. I—I've gotten to know Richard, and he's so, well, honest and kind." She stopped, puzzled by the intensity of her own feeling and also tripped up by the word *honest*. Why had Richard not told her who he was, even as they had talked about Rena and the resort? Had he been ashamed of his mother? He had warned her about getting involved. Did he suspect Harry all along? Did he know something about Rena's predicament?

Perhaps there were many reasons why people kept secrets. She herself had not talked to Richard about her calling and work among the people back home. She hadn't told him that she was running from them, from the terrible pain of failure. Indeed, the reasons people withheld truth were not clearly defined in her own mind. Angie walked faster, drawing Rena along.

"I wonder if they know that we're gone yet," Angie ventured as she stepped into the clearing along the road. "We've made it. It won't be far to town now."

Rena's great strain was visible in the increased light. She was perspiring but still shivering, and a sickly pallor surrounded the blueness of her eyes. Angie was suddenly afraid. Maybe she had made a mistake dragging her out. Perhaps she should have gone for help alone and returned for Rena.

"Aunt Rena, what is it? Are you sick? Is there something else?"

"I'm a diabetic, Angie. I have been for a long time. But I think I took my medicine this morning—"

"You think?" Angie stopped and searched Rena's face.

"Well, Lenore usually reminds me—" The childish tremor

had crept back into her voice. She dropped her head as though she had disappointed a parent.

"Well, never mind. We'll get you settled soon and you'll be taken care of," she said with an assurance she did not feel. "Dear Lord," she whispered into the dark sky, "please let someone come along!"

Hardly had the prayer passed from her lips when lights from an approaching car lit up the road. The car streamed by them, then suddenly slowed and pulled over as Angie hurried toward it, clutching Rena's arm.

They had almost reached the car when Rena gasped.

"It's okay, Aunt Rena, come on."

"But Angie, it's—it's—"

Too late Angie realized what Rena was trying to say. A little man in baggy pants was hauling himself out of the car. Moonlight shone on his bald head, giving it a sickly yellow glow, and his little eyes shone like beads.

"Ladies, you shouldn't be out on such a dreadful night," he said, clicking teeth that shone as yellow as his bald head. "Come now, I'll take you home." He opened the rear door and bowed low in a mock gesture, extending his stubby fingers.

Angie and Rena instinctively backed up. Angie had mistrusted this little man from the first moment she had seen him when he had come with a message for Jen. She had wondered vaguely at the time why a message was necessary when there were phones in every cabin. At the time she had been surprised and disgusted with herself for that initial reaction to Tinker and for her lack of charity.

Now she said politely, "We're on our way to town, Mr. Tinker. Thanks just the same, but we'll walk." She moved away with Rena.

Tinker stepped sideways with amazing speed, blocking their passage. The muscles of his face, level now with Angie's, rippled into a hard, sardonic smile. He whipped something from his pocket, something shiny and too large in the dwarfed hand. A second later Angie felt its cold intrusion against her side, penetrating her coat and chilling her heart.

"My God, Tinker, put that thing away! What do you think you're—" It was Rena's voice, aghast, paternal.

"I prefer your friend's manner of speakin'," came the steely response. "It's Mister Tinker. Remember that—*Mister!* Now get in the car, if you want to see your polite friend stay healthy!"

Angie felt another hard thrust of the gun in her ribs as she climbed woodenly into the back seat. In a flash the awful images of her dream came pouring before her eyes: Eddie, chasing the huge crimson and yellow butterfly, chasing it to the edge of the precipice and dropping over, again and again. Little Eddies dropping over, smiles turned to streaks of horror on tender faces.

The same horror engulfed her now. This couldn't be happening! Not here. Not now. Somehow actual evil is always more insidious than a person could ever imagine. Would she ever see Jen or anyone she loved ever again? If only this too were some kind of evil dream from which she would awaken.

The little man began to whistle through his teeth, a nameless, dreadful tune. He deftly turned the old car around and drove in the direction of Pinewood Acres.

eighteen

Truth, crushed to earth, shall rise again;
Th' eternal years of God are hers;
But Error, wounded, writhes in pain,
And dies among his worshippers.

WILLIAM CULLEN BRYANT

The rain had stopped, but thunder groaned throaty and low, like the discontented grumblings of old men. That, coupled with Tinker's tuneless whistling, produced an unbearable tension in Angie. She felt her heart clawing inside like a trapped animal. On the seat beside her Rena wrung her hands again and again, warming her chilled fingers, or perhaps trying to render them still, for she was trembling all over.

Angie closed her hand over Rena's and gave it a firm squeeze. Then she turned her attention to the front seat, to the unkempt gray hair. A beaten plaid cap obscured Tinker's baldness, but through the rearview mirror his restless eyes in their little round sockets met Angie's. Their coldness made her shiver.

"Mrs. Mara needs a doctor, Tinker—uh, Mr. Tinker—" She worked to keep her voice level.

"I told you I was taking you home. Call yourself a doctor then," he said, "though it appears to me you might have thought of that a'fore you lit out in the rain and cold and all." He gave a mirthless little laugh and began to whistle again.

"Why are you doing this?" Angie demanded.

"Why, I told you. I picked you up because you'd catch your death in this rain!"

"You know what I mean," she stammered in angry frustration. "You—"

"You're beginning to lose your manners, Miss Carlson, them fine manners of yours," the man quipped with hostility through his clicking teeth. "And I'm tired of your questions. Ask Riggs. He might tell you, if he's a mind to."

Tinker said no more; even the whistling ceased. And as they sped along the winding road, the tension grew. It would have been impossible to jump out, even if she were certain that he wouldn't use that gun, the cold pressure of which was still strong in her memory, so strong that she could almost feel it pressed against her side.

The car slowed; Angie could see through the rain-spattered window that they had arrived at Rena's house and were winding up the long driveway to the stone mansion. Then Tinker sped up suddenly, swung sharply around the corner, and stopped at the rear of the house.

"Get out!" he ordered, turning around and glaring at them through his small, menacing eyes.

Angie helped Rena out onto the porous ground, bracing herself against the cold metal of the car.

"Inside!" He held the gun ludicrously in his pudgy hand and shooed them through the back door as though they were chickens being herded into the henhouse.

Once inside, Tinker secured the lock and turned to them. "Now, why don't you have a seat around the table. If you please!" Tinker set his thick frame down on one of the chairs and drew his leathery lips into a petulant pucker. He scratched his head with the barrel of his revolver as he watched them sit obediently down.

What a stupid little man, scratching his head with the gun! What if the thing should go off? Angie grimaced. If only she had the courage to call his bluff! The gun was probably a dimestore toy. Maybe.

Rena gave a miserable groan as she sat down, and her head appeared to fall forward onto her chest. Angie went over to her quickly, removed her own coat, and placed it over Rena's shivering body.

Poor Rena. She seemed so much thinner and older. Had she taken her medicine that day? What was a diabetic coma like? Was Aunt Rena in danger of such a catastrophe? Or was Rena suffering from a combination of blood sugar problems and alcohol abuse?

Suddenly growing bold in her concern for her friend, Angie moved apart and groped for a light switch.

"No light," Tinker sputtered, blocking Angie's way with his fat shoulder.

"What is the matter with you?" she demanded, looking Tinker full in the face. Moonlight glimmered through the kitchen window and showed up dark encrustings of dirt in the lines of his fat face. "Don't you see that she's ill? We need to call her doctor. She can't be held here like some kind of prisoner—"

A car coming to a quick halt outside ended the confrontation. Angie held her breath as a key turned in the lock. Tinker bounded to the door with the alacrity of a dog going to meet its master.

Suddenly Harrington Riggs stood framed in the doorway; a pale Lenore craned her neck behind him. The two entered quickly, secretively. Lenore, dressed in black with a wine-colored raincoat flung over her angular shoulders, closed the door behind them. Riggs shook rain from his hat and brushed Tinker aside with one sweep of his great arm.

Riggs's usual suave grin covered his flushed face, and beneath reddish brows his eyes sparkled in cold humor. "I see you've found our lost friends," he said with a sardonic glance in Tinker's direction. "Ah, but why haven't you made them more comfortable! Tinker, I'm ashamed of you."

Tinker cringed and frowned. He slunk back and propped himself up against the far wall near the fireplace.

Riggs deftly switched on a hanging lamp that swayed over the table and bowed slightly to Angie who hovered over Rena, securing her coat around the older woman's shoulders. "Please, Miss Carlson, won't you sit down?"

"I do not want to sit down," she began with a boldness that surprised her. "And we do not wish to remain here. I demand to know why we're being held here."

Harrington Riggs pretended he heard nothing. He stroked his jaw as he gave Rena a scrutinizing glance. "My dear Mrs. Mara, I should have thought you'd learned to take better care of yourself by now." He turned to Lenore, who looked paler than death. "Do get her a drink," he finished with a twinge of disgust in his smooth tones.

"No!" Angie shouted. "She doesn't need a drink. She needs a doctor, and I'm going to get her one . . . now!" She pressed toward the telephone on the wall.

Tinker was there in a second, pointing the gun directly at her. Angie froze.

"Harry! You promised!" It was Lenore, fairly screaming and clutching Riggs's arm with her long tapered fingers. Imploringly she looked from him to Rena with a horrified expression.

"Tinker, are you still playing with that thing?" Riggs remonstrated as though scolding a child. "Put it away. There's no need." He was chillingly in control, the implacable smile dripping like melted jelly from his face.

"Miss Carlson, you've no need to concern yourself." Riggs raised an eyebrow. "Tinker gets carried away sometimes with his own heroics. He's harmless really, a mere child."

He paused and then turned cold eyes on her. "I've arranged for Lenore to take you directly to the airport. Your things will be sent on to you. You see, we've found it necessary to rent your cabin to another client. According to our agreement your time is up. I've taken the liberty of checking out for you. I'm sure you understand."

Incredulous, Angie stared at him, riveted to her spot on the floor. "No, I don't understand. I don't understand at all." But Riggs paid no attention to her remonstrances.

"There's just one little item of business to be completed," Riggs continued. "Ah, yes, here it is." He pulled a triple-folded document from his shirt pocket and shook it out against his broad chest. "Once we take care of this, Lenore will call Mrs. Mara's personal physician immediately."

How could he possibly hope to get away with this? It was incredible. Angie stared at the document, at the implacable Riggs. It had to be the agreement he had tried to get Aunt Rena to sign before, the deed to her property.

"I also have a check drawn up—right here—in the amount of two hundred thousand—just as we agreed, Mrs. Mara. It—" he paused ever so slightly, "it seems we really must get on with this now." He took a step toward Rena and held the pen toward her. Rena watched with wide eyes too weary to show her outrage. "I'm sure you don't mind. Miss

Carlson here can witness our agreement."

Angie found her voice. "A contract signed under duress won't stand up in court," she said with amazement.

"Duress? I'm sure you're quite mistaken, my dear child. Mrs. Mara knows we've her best interests at heart. She herself agrees that the resort has become a burden to her." A dark look creased his face, but it quickly evaporated. He held out the pen. "Mrs. Mara . . . if you please."

Rena took the pen with trembling fingers. Her face, pale in startling contrast to her copper-colored hair, had an inscrutable expression.

"Aunt Rena, you don't have to sign that." Angie placed her hand on the older woman's shoulder. "You don't have to sell out."

"Angie, dear, I'm tired, tired of all this business. I'm too old to run a resort. Harry's price is a fair one. I've—I've no desire to keep this place anymore."

Angie was shocked by the ludicrous nature of the situation and by Rena's lack of spirit. "But Aunt Rena, you—you—" she stuttered, frantic to dissuade her. "You don't even know that this check is valid! Think what you're doing. Is this any way for an honest man to conduct business?"

Rena spoke with sudden maturity and surprising steadiness. "We have no choice, really. Harry is not above doing anything necessary to get what he wants. I'll not have you hurt." Her blue eyes, shiny now with tears and weariness and illness, touched Angie with singular affection.

Riggs pointed to the contract, urging Rena to sign. A night bird called mournfully outside the window. It seemed to make him edgy, and his eyes darted around the room and out the wide window toward the veranda. He nodded to

Lenore. "Lenore, help Mrs. Mara with the papers."

She pressed her immaculately groomed fingers against each other in an incongruous gesture that looked like prayer and then with resignation brushed past Riggs. She bent over Rena's trembling fingers. Riggs looked on with narrowed eyes, his arms folded across his expansive chest.

A sound, at first like wind in the rushes, then more like the soft tread of a man's feet, startled them all. Then to everyone's surprise, a polite knock sounded.

Riggs flashed Tinker a look that set the little man on guard but at the same time checked his manner. Lenore took the other chair and lit a cigarette with unsure hands. Riggs put the contract back into his pocket and quietly opened the door.

There in the moonlight, tall, stern, and looking like a golden knight more noble than any who rode with King Arthur, was Richard Ogden.

A surge of joy flooded Angie's heart. "Richard!"

His eyes, piercing in their blueness, softened momentarily as they fell on her and then on the face of his mother. Then quickly he stepped inside to face Harry Riggs.

"What's going on here, Riggs?" he asked, holding the man in a steady gaze.

"I'm afraid your mother and Miss Carlson here lost their way. My man, Tinker, was good enough to give them a ride back to Pinewood." His suave command of himself was incredible.

"We weren't lost!" Angie broke in, only to be suddenly silenced in Riggs's continuing barrage of words.

"Mrs. Mara foolishly struck out on her own in this cold rain. I'm sure you understand that she doesn't always act in her own best interests. As I said, luckily enough Tinker was driving along and kindly returned her home. I assure you your mother is quite all right, assuming that is a genuine concern of yours." The caustic words stung the air.

Richard turned from him and stepped close to the chair where Rena sat. His eyes focused solemnly on his mother as he answered Riggs's accusation with gentle authority. "It *is* a concern, a great concern."

Several seconds of silence ensued as though some great thing were transpiring that suspended all other action in the universe.

"She was going to sign over the resort to Harry—for two hundred thousand dollars!" Angie burst out.

Richard turned back to the manager. "Two hundred thousand, a tidy sum considering that you built that particular fortune by extortion!"

Rena gasped. Riggs turned from pale gray to crimson.

"That's right. You're offering to buy Pinewood Acres with the money you've been bilking out of it for five years. Isn't that about right, Mr. Riggs?"

"That sir, is a libelous statement and one that could get you into a great deal of trouble, even more trouble than breaking and entering," Riggs said darkly.

"Perhaps," Richard said, intent now on Lenore, whose face was as pale as moonlight. Her eyes turned downward, and her long tapered fingers knotted and twisted around her cigarette.

"Except," Richard continued, "that it isn't libel, but truth." He fixed his eyes on Lenore. "My mother might have come to understand this long ago had her personal mail not been intercepted." He paused and deliberately drew an envelope from his inside pocket.

All eyes followed his movement. The stillness closed

around them taut, unbending.

"I found this when I was going through some things here. I was looking for a clue to mother's sudden disappearance." Richard paused. "I believe you said she was off to visit a sister. Wasn't that it, Lenore?"

But Lenore drew steadily on her cigarette, staring away from him as the coils of smoke ringed the air.

"This is the last letter I wrote to Mother, three months ago. It's still unopened."

"Your personal business, I assure you, is of no concern here," Riggs quipped. "Now if you don't mind—"

"Oh, but I do."

"Richard?" It was Rena's voice, strained, unfamiliar. "A letter from you, Richard?"

"Yes, mother. I wrote many. I thought you knew."

Lenore's eyelids fluttered and dropped. "I—I know how you felt about him. I . . . was only protecting you," she stammered. "You told me that all he cared about was your money." She nervously smoked her cigarette.

"Don't you see, Aunt Rena, they've been using you, playing up your hurt over Richard," Angie said then. "And all the time he's been wanting to prove that he cared about you."

Riggs buttoned his jacket, puffing out his chest self-consciously. "Well, all this sentimentality is a bit too much at this hour. Lenore, let's get a breath of air. Tinker, it's past your bedtime, too."

As the three started for the door, it was suddenly opened for them, and two men filled the entrance, badges gleaming silver in the moonlight. Riggs stared in total surprise, silent as the Castor County Sheriff informed him of his arrest.

"We ran that check, Ogden," the sheriff said in a calm

even voice. "Seems Mr. Riggs here is in some demand over in Lane County."

Angie stared as the authorities took Harrington away. Lenore's cigarette had burned away to a tiny stub that she continued to hold in her fingers as she stared with an expression of anguish. Angie felt desperately sorry for her. Lenore stumbled after the men, as though she too would be taken into custody, for where else had she to go now? Perhaps soon enough she too would be implicated. But they drove away, leaving her standing in the rain, her hair blowing in the wind like a roll of black steam.

Tinker cowered in the corner of Rena's kitchen, covering his eyes with his stubby fingers. His lips were mouthing words, but no sounds came. Even when he, like Lenore, had been warned by the sheriff not to leave town, he had made no response but had merely nodded with a quivering motion that was more like a sob.

"Mother." Richard stood above her, one arm tentatively shielding her shoulder. "Are you all right?"

Angie came near them, sensing that she was an intruder in the sweet tension of the moment. Perhaps she shouldn't be witnessing this uncommon reunion. But she spoke for Rena, who seemed unable to respond.

"I think we need to take her to a hospital immediately. She's had a rough evening, and she's not sure if she took her insulin this morning. See how pallid she is, how her pulse races."

"Insulin is only part of the problem," Rena whispered shakily. "I need a drink, but I don't want one! Not really. I—Oh, God, I do want it, but I want to be free of it. I'll—I'll do anything!" She paused and turned anguished eyes on Angie. "Is it true what you said about hope, Angie? For me?"

"Oh, yes, Aunt Rena!" Angie's heart leaped with joy as she realized that Aunt Rena had come to the point of real change in her life. Thank God, she said without words, sensing the nearly palpable presence of the One who is hope and light and soundness. His peace seemed to cover them, enfold them, even as the terror and the uncertainty had shaken them so violently only moments ago. Strange what happenings could fill a moment! Strange how penetrating the Peacemaker's touch upon them all!

"We're going to get help for you, Mother. It will be all right." He knelt by her and soothed her gently. He looked up into Angie's face. "Thank God for you, Angie," he whispered as his arm tightened around his mother. "Yes, we'll drive to the hospital right now. Will you come, Angie?"

There was such tenderness in his voice and in the appeal of his moist, blue eyes that she could not speak, only nod her willingness. Where suspicion, coldness, and silence had chained these two, the warmth of love and truth had torn away the chains and left them melded by a greater bond.

As they left the mansion, the dogs, who had been such menacing beasts before, now whined pitifully in the night, as though sensing something of tragedy, of import, and of love.

nineteen

Sail on, nor fear to breast the sea!
Our hearts, our hopes, are all with thee
Our hearts, our hopes, our prayers, our tears,
Our faith triumphant o'er our fears,
Are all with thee—are all with thee!

HENRY WADSWORTH LONGFELLOW

In the hospital waiting room Angie poured herself a cup of coffee and walked to the window. She watched the moonlight play on the mimosa boughs scraping the window. They rustled with a subtle sadness, as though they remembered their first spring, as though summer would not soon fade and the gentle winds no long caress them.

Then she saw her own reflection in the glass, the same willowy figure, the same deep-set eyes and light brown hair, but yet not the same, not the same as when she had meditated on her reflection that first day at Pinewood Acres, consumed with her failure and with sorrow for her lost ones.

The woman looking back at her was older somehow, wiser and settled. Perhaps that was as it should be, for she had made her decision. Maybe it had happened in the coffee shop when she watched life trembling in her cup and sensed so totally the presence of Christ. Maybe it had happened when Rena had unwittingly spoken the healing word to her, the word she needed at that moment. Or maybe it was the smudged letter from Roslyn Loss,

Eddie's sister. It had come only hours before she had found Rena locked in her room and this long night of terrors and wonders had begun.

A short message, scrawled on a half sheet of notebook paper, had said that Mrs. Loss, Roslyn's mother, was going to die. The cancer treatments were no longer working. "I'm scared. I wish you were here" ended the letter, which was signed "Rosie." No one had ever called her that, but it was the name that she preferred.

When Angie finished reading the letter, she folded it carefully and placed it in her purse with a strange sense of calm. Only days earlier she would have thrown up her hands in despair. Wasn't it enough that Eddie was dead, murdered, that Roslyn had little chance to get out of the ghetto she lived in? Now their mother would be taken, too. She agonized for Roslyn and yet—yet there was hope! Nothing was beyond Him, He who loved this sad woman-child and who had a plan for her life.

Yes, she had decided to go back, but she would be quite different than when she had left. She smiled at her reflection in the window now, wondering about it all, eager to find Roslyn and to tell her about hope and the love that could never be taken from her. Whatever else life held for Angie, she knew that she must return now.

It was closer to daybreak than to midnight, and the waiting room was empty except for the stillness and the night spilling in through the window. Angie turned to see Richard standing in the doorway, his blue eyes serious yet enigmatic. He ran a hand through his hair and dropped both hands loosely into the pockets of his gray slacks. He stood looking at her.

"She's going to be all right, thanks to you," he said quietly. "The alcoholism treatment is going to be a challenge, but I believe she's ready now, and I think the thanks goes to you for that also, Angie."

She looked away, embarrassed by his tender gratitude.

"You gave her hope and showed her genuine care. Angie, I—well—I'm sorry. I should have told you who I was from the start. I was ashamed, afraid of what you'd think of me."

"It's all right, Richard. I understand."

"I hope you can forgive me," he broke in. The look in his eyes was so full of pain and pleading that Angie hastened to reassure him.

"If you can forgive me for what I thought! That night in the woods when I was being chased over the bridge, and I saw your coat . . . well, I began to believe that you really were what Harry and Lenore said and what Aunt Rena thought. I didn't want to believe it. It just didn't seem possible. You were so—" She stopped herself, turned and faced the dark window.

There was silence as he stepped into the little room and moved toward her. He stopped behind her, close enough so that she could smell the aroma of his after-shave. The memories of the balloon fair and the exhilarating skyride settled warmly around her like an unexpected wave of tropical air.

"These have been some of the best days of my life, Angie," he said quietly.

She turned and met his eyes, blue and flecked with sunlight like a summer sky. "I've enjoyed them, too, Richard." She sighed softly then and moved to the little coffee counter stocked for the convenience of visitors.

"Can I pour you some?" she asked.

"Angie—"

"Richard," she interrupted, not trusting her own quickening pulse. How easy it would be to love this man, to let him absorb all future failure, hurt, or bewilderment. She knew that he cared about her, that the slightest move toward him. . . . "I haven't exactly been honest with you either. I—I never told you about myself, about my work. You see, for the last four years I have been youth minister in an inner-city mission."

His lips curved into a knowing smile, and his eyes held hers warmly. "I'm not in the least surprised. I knew you were, well, really special. I know you helped me to finally settle things with the Lord."

"Oh, Richard." The light in his face was truly the light of God, the light that bursts forth in a life with a singular radiance. It was the way she had seen him when he had walked into the kitchen at the mansion to face Harry . . . like a golden knight.

"It was you, Angie, and what you said that day in the balloon. That's what finally clinched it. I'd read and reread the Scriptures until I could practically quote them, but I couldn't bring myself to believe. Then, there was this bird crying—a seagull—and it was soaring restlessly in its search for water. It couldn't find the ocean and . . . well, I know it sounds silly, but I knew that if it would only drop down to the lake it would find what it needed. I knew that I simply had to put my faith down and believe. I . . . did that. Thank God He was willing to forgive me and to save me."

Never did a testimony fill Angie with such joy. And to think that God had allowed her to have some little part. "I didn't tell you about myself," she said, "because, well, because I had been considering not going back."

Richard's eyebrows drew together in a puzzled frown as they faced each other in the dim light.

She walked away a little and began to tell him about those she had loved and worked with, about how hard it had been, about her struggles with her failures and with the sense of being too small to cope with the stresses of it all.

"You see, I had spent four years there and nothing—no one—" She stopped as her eyes filled with tears and the pain caught in her throat. "Their suffering is so intense, Richard, and I—I couldn't seem to help them."

The horrid dream flashed before her once again: the mesmerized eyes, great and brown like smoldering coals in the thin face; the twisted little smile as the butterfly, all crimson and silver, sallied and bobbed in the strange darkness; the cliff and Roslyn stumbling toward it unknowing, unconcerned, delighted, bewitched.

Did the horror in her eyes frighten Richard? His face became pale and he closed his hand over hers. "Tell me about it, Angie," he said gently.

She poured it all out like spilled lemonade from a pitcher held in childish, unpracticed hands. All the fearful feelings of inferiority, the wondering, the longing came out. And he listened quietly with averted eyes. When she finished she took the handkerchief he held out to her.

"I've needed to talk about this for a long time. I think everything that has happened here has helped me a great deal. I mean, Aunt Rena, well, she was like so many I have worked with . . . and now she's going to be all right and . . . it's given me hope that maybe I can—" She stopped as though a new thought had come to her.

"I know I shouldn't look for signs or even expect that people will always make the right decisions. It's God who's working after all. I'm only His instrument. Yes, that's it! I'd lost sight of that and thought it was all up to me. I know it sounds silly." She rose, tucking Richard's handkerchief into her pocket. She walked away toward the window.

"Look, Richard, the rain has stopped, and the moon is so bright it's like daylight." She tugged at his hand and drew him to the window.

"Angie?" He spoke her name softly and with a question. "When are you going back?"

"Tomorrow," she responded quickly, the light still shining in her eyes. "I'll leave word for Jen and take the train. That way I'll be there in time for Sunday."

She stopped, aware of the sadness in Richard's eyes, and of her own sadness, for she knew she would miss him profoundly. She had not dared to let herself hope that they might one day belong to each other. Perhaps in the back of her heart that romantic girlish longing that never quite leaves a woman sheltered its dream. But she had been given a trust, and it must be fulfilled.

"Can I write to you?" he asked simply, his hands still deep in his pockets, as though clinging to something steady there.

"I hope you will," she said softly.

Resolutely he pulled his hands out and clasped them around hers as he looked her full in the face. "Angie, I won't tell you that I don't want to throw my arms around you and carry you away with me. But I owe you much more than that, more than I can offer now. And I don't want to lose you. Do you understand that, Angie?" he whispered.

She nodded, her heart too full for speech.

"There's another thing you have to understand, too," he said, lowering his eyes now and fixing his gaze on their clasped hands. "I—I had a wife. We were divorced five years ago . . . one more thing I never told you."

"It's all right, Richard. You don't have to—"

"Strange what demands the truth makes on a man," he said.

Angie pulled away gently and faced the window. There was no reason he should have told her. They were so new to each other. Yet from the moment in the balloon she had felt him almost a part of her that would always be, no matter how far or how long she traveled. Perhaps that was why she ached, now when all logic argued against her feeling.

"My former wife was an alcoholic like my mother. She wouldn't let me help her. She wouldn't listen. She didn't want to be married to me anymore." He paced a little before taking a steadying breath and facing her again. "I've never been interested in anyone since then . . . until you."

The hissing of the coffee pot and the mechanical click from the heating plate filled the tense moment. Angie was drawn by the tenderness in his eyes and by the dawning in her heart of love that could not be forced away.

"So, knowing all that, will you let me keep in touch with you, Angie?"

"Oh, Richard, nothing would make me happier!" And she entered the warm circle of his arms. They stood for several timeless moments, held in an embrace tighter than physical closeness. Somewhere near the window a mourning dove crooned in the stillness, a sweet song full of mystery and longing, a sweet half-song, not yet complete.

"Come," Richard said tenderly. "I'll take you back to Pinewood Acres. You must get some rest."

Angie hooked her arm through Richard's and let him lead her from the hospital.

"I'm going to be sticking around to get things on an even keel at the resort and to be with Mother." Richard's voice seemed at one with the departing night and the slow creeping in of dawn.

"You'll need a new manager now," Angie said, remembering the practical implications of all that the night had held.

"Yes, and there's the legal mess. But I'm going to see that Mother has a good business running when the treatment is over. She's put so much into that place."

"Yes, and it's so beautiful here!"

"I want it to be that way when you come to Pinewood next summer! Of course I'll keep you filled in on all the details, and on what happens to Lenore and poor old Tinker. Mother really was rather fond of that man, although I can't imagine why. As for Lenore, it's really sad that she got sidetracked by Riggs and that Mother had to suffer for it. Lenore never really wanted to hurt Mother. I really believe that."

"Perhaps so," Angie mused. "It has been quite a vacation, certainly nothing like I had planned. For instance, I never expected to meet you. Strange what turn events can take." She grinned at Richard and they walked together to the car.

Later in the morning he would drive her to the train and watch as it carried her away. Her mind's vision of him standing there suddenly filled her with an enormous sadness. Would she ever see him again? Would they ever again walk like this, hand in hand, safe with each other, comfortable, while morning wakened with soft promises in an unfulfilled sky?

Another vision came quietly, deep in the center of her being. She sat in the campfire ring, gazing as the sparks flew upward, sparks of vibrant life, electric, directed. The sureness, the pure sense of being herself, alive and directed by God, enveloped her. This too she could trust to Him, to Him who was her life.

A Letter To Our Readers

Dear Reader:

In order that we might better contribute to your reading enjoyment, we would appreciate your taking a few minutes to respond to the following questions and return to:

Karen Carroll, Editor
Heartsong Presents
P.O. Box 719
Uhrichsville, Ohio 44683

1. Did you enjoy reading *This Trembling Cup*?
   - ❑ Very much. I would like to see more books by this author!
   - ❑ Moderately
   - ❑ I would have enjoyed it more if

   ____

2. Where did you purchase this book? ____________

   ____

3. What influenced your decision to purchase this book?

❑ Cover	❑ Back cover copy
❑ Title	❑ Friends
❑ Publicity	❑ Other

4. Please rate the following elements from 1 (poor) to 10 (superior).
   - ❑ Heroine ❑ Plot
   - ❑ Hero ❑ Inspirational theme
   - ❑ Setting ❑ Secondary characters
5. What settings would you like to see in Heartsong Presents Books?

   ____

   ____
6. What are some inspirational themes you would like to see treated in future books?

   ____

   ____
7. Would you be interested in reading other Heartsong Presents books?
   - ❑ Very interested
   - ❑ Moderately interested
   - ❑ Not interested
8. Please indicate your age range:
   - ❑ Under 18 ❑ 25-34 ❑ 46-55
   - ❑ 18-24 ❑ 35-45 ❑ Over 55

Name ___________________________________

Occupation ______________________________

Address _________________________________

City ______________ State ______ Zip ________